פִּרְקֵי אָבוֹת

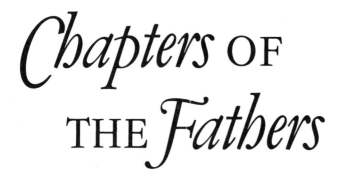

Chapters OF
THE *Fathers*

TRANSLATION & COMMENTARY *by*
SAMSON RAPHAEL HIRSCH

New, corrected Edition

The Samson Raphael Hirsch Publications Society

FELDHEIM PUBLISHERS · Jerusalem

Second, corrected edition

ISBN 0 87306 182 9

Rendered into English by
GERTRUDE HIRSCHLER

Copyright © 1967, 1979 by
FELDHEIM PUBLISHERS, Ltd.
POB 6525 / Jerusalem, Israel

Distributed in the United States of America by

PHILIPP FELDHEIM, INC.
"THE HOUSE OF THE JEWISH BOOK"
96 East Broadway, New York 10002

ביצוע א.ג.פ. שרותים לאופסט, ירושלים

Printed in Israel

FOREWORD

Rabbi Samson Raphael Hirsch's Commentary to the "Chapters of the Fathers" is taken from his commentary to the Tefilla. This explains its relative brevity. It had to be concise in order to fit within the contours of the work. The author set for himself the task of analyzing and illuminating the truths which permeate our Tefilla and are of decisive importance for our Jewish lives. Since our Tefilla constitutes the most faithful reflection of the truths gleaned from Tanach, it is only natural that Rav Hirsch presupposed the reader's familiarity with his great commentary to Tanach and consequently limited himself to a form of summary or synopsis in his Tefilla commentary.

The same consideration determined the scope of his comments to the "Chapters of the Fathers." For the ethical truths and demands laid down in these chapters are in no way new truths or new demands. Not once do the prophets and the singers and poets of our sacred writings who are imbued with the spirit of God proclaim a new message of truth; they drew every truth and demand directly from God's Torah and saw their task solely in guiding their people to the Torah and towards its faithful fulfilment. In exactly the same vein, all the teachings and admonitions, all precepts of ethical truth to whose adherence the "Fathers" exhort their people, are borne by the spirit with which the sacred sources of Tanach inspire and shape our Jewish thinking and doing.

The Commentary to the Tefilla was the final chapter in Rav Hirsch's blessed literary life work and it was published posthumously. The translation of the works of this immortal teacher and leader of our people into a vernacular (Hebrew, English) which will make them accessible to the Jewish masses at large proves ever more an urgent necessity. The fact that a large part of Hirschian literature has already been translated — having been received with tremendous enthusiasm — justifies the hope that the remaining works not yet published in English and the large part of the Hirsch literature as yet untranslated into *loshon hakodesh*, especially the Chumash, will become available in the not too distant future. The present translation of the פרקי אבות is a further welcome step in this direction להגדיל תורה ולהאדירה.

New York City, Tishri 5727   RABBI DR. JOSEPH BREUER

Chapters of the Fathers | פרקי אבות

פרקי אבות

From Pesach *till* Rosh Hashanah *a chapter of* Pirkei Avoth *is read each* Sabbath *after* Minchah.

כָּל יִשְׂרָאֵל יֵשׁ לָהֶם חֵלֶק לְעוֹלָם הַבָּא, שֶׁנֶּאֱמַר וְעַמֵּךְ כֻּלָּם

צַדִּיקִים לְעוֹלָם יִירְשׁוּ אָרֶץ נֵצֶר מַטָּעַי מַעֲשֵׂה יָדַי לְהִתְפָּאֵר:

כל ישראל. **עולם הבא** denotes a two-fold future; one in the world to come, and one in this world. The future in the world to come is that bliss into which the soul of man enters when, immediately after the death of the body, it departs from earth. The future in this world is the coming of the kingdom of felicity, perfection and peace which God will establish on earth; it is the final purpose of all human progress and development. **כל ישראל** Any individual who remains worthy of the name of *Yisrael* and who has not utterly divorced himself from Israel's lofty spiritual and ethical destiny and task has a portion in both of these—in the future of the world to come as well as in that of the world here below. His portion may vary depending on his degree of loyalty to Israel's task and destiny, but as long as he will remain *Yisrael* he will never lose it entirely. Whatever good we achieve in loyal obedience to God here below becomes a spiritual accomplishment which will accompany us into the world to come and into the presence of our Father in Heaven. At the same time it serves as still another seedling sown into the field of mankind's future with which we add to the total of the harvest of what is good and pleasing in the sight of God, a sowing which will ripen one day into salvation for mankind on earth and through which we attain immortality even here below.

The expression **ירש ארץ** appears in the Psalms and in Prophetic literature to denote that two-fold future which may be inherited by virtue of a life of

SAYINGS OF THE FATHERS

All Israel have a portion in the world to come, as it is said, "Thy people, all of them righteous, shall inherit the earth forever, the flower of My repeated plantings, the work of My hands, to glorify Me."

---

loyal obedience on earth, and which becomes the inheritance of the righteous since the unfaithful have forfeited it by their disregard of their duty. (See Comm. Psalms Notes to Psalm 25:13, 37:22 et al.) שנאמר: (Isaiah 60:21), נצר מטעי, the goal of universal moral perfection and bliss proclaimed in these verses will not materialize all at once. God will plant and replant His people over and over again, as it were, until it will finally be ripe for that future salvation, at which time it will stand confirmed as the uniform work of God made for His glorification.

Actually, the verse beginning with כל ישראל is not part of Pirkei Avoth but is taken from the Mishnah (Sanhedrin 90a) where it serves to introduce the final portion of the Tractate. It is placed here as an introduction to Pirkei Avoth because it outlines the great goal for which the maxims contained in these *Perakim* are intended to strengthen and train us and because, at the same time, it furnishes added incentive to all to apply themselves vigorously to the pursuit of that goal which is within the reach of all. It is most appropriate, then, that the sages of our Law should be referred to in these passages as *Avoth*, for with these sayings they truly act as our "fathers", providing us, in their discerning wisdom, with the ethical guidance we need to attain the state of perfection ordained for us by God.

א מֹשֶׁה קִבֵּל תּוֹרָה מִסִּינַי, וּמְסָרָהּ לִיהוֹשֻׁעַ וִיהוֹשֻׁעַ לִזְקֵנִים
וּזְקֵנִים לִנְבִיאִים וּנְבִיאִים מְסָרוּהָ לְאַנְשֵׁי כְנֶסֶת הַגְּדוֹלָה · הֵם
אָמְרוּ שְׁלֹשָׁה דְבָרִים, הֱווּ מְתוּנִים בַּדִּין וְהַעֲמִידוּ תַלְמִידִים
הַרְבֵּה וַעֲשׂוּ סְיָג לַתּוֹרָה :

---

1. **מסיני**. As Wessely explains in יין לבנון, his commentary to *Pirkei Avoth*, "Sinai" is the historic event of the Giving of the Law which took place in the sight and hearing of the entire Jewish people. In this manner, the Divine origin of the Law that came to us through Moses was established as a certainty through personal experience which permanently rules out all doubt and is not part of belief but of actual knowledge. "Behold, I am coming to you," God told Moses (Exod. 19:9) "in a thick cloud so that the people may hear when I speak with you, and then they will also believe you forever." You yourselves have seen," we read in Exod. 20:22, "that I have spoken with you from Heaven." "These words", we further read in Deut. 5:19–24, "God spoke to all your assembly on the mountain out of the midst of the fire, of the cloud and of the thick darkness...and you came near to me, all the heads of your tribes and your elders, and you said, 'Behold, God, our God, has let us see His glory and His greatness and we have heard His voice out of the midst of the fire; we have seen this day that God spoke to man and he remained alive. And now why should we die that this great fire should consume us...You go near and hear all that God, our God, may say to you;...we will hear it and do it.'" "Only take heed to yourself and guard your soul exceedingly, lest you forget the facts which your eyes have seen, and lest they depart from your heart all the days of your life; and make them known to your children and your children's children; the day when you stood before God, your God, in Horeb, when God said to me: 'Assemble Me the people and I will make them hear My words that they may learn to fear Me all the days that they live upon the earth and that they may teach their children.'" (Deut. 4:9–10) "To you it was shown that you might know, הראת לדעת, that God is God alone; there is none else beside Him. Out of Heaven He made you hear His voice in order to discipline you..." (Deut. 4:35–36)

It is the direct character of this Divine revelation that the term *Misinai* is intended to recall, for it should bring to mind the Divine origin of the Law and its preservation by way of a process of transmission carried on from age to age and through the leaders of each generation. משה קבל. Moses received the Law from the Lord on Mount Sinai in the full view of all the people and expounded it to the people during the forty years of their wanderings through the wilderness. But then, before he died, *mosar*—he "handed it over" to

1.   Moshe received the Torah from Sinai and handed it down to Yehoshua; Yehoshua to the Elders; the Elders to the Prophets; the Prophets handed it down to the Men of the Great Assembly. The latter said three things: Be cautious in judgment, raise up many disciples and make a fence for the Law.

Joshua to ensure its perpetuation through study and observance. With the same purpose in mind, Joshua, in turn, handed over the Law to the Elders who survived and succeeded him. (Joshua 24:31) From these the Prophets took over the task of guarding and protecting the Torah. Eventually, when the Jewish exiles returned from Babylonian captivity and the building of the Second Temple was begun in Jerusalem, the place of the Prophets was taken by "The Men of the Great Assembly", a body of one hundred and twenty members. Haggai, Zechariah and Malachi, the last of the Prophets, were among the members of this group. According to the Sages, (Yoma 69b) this "great" Assembly proved its "greatness" primarily by its ability to comprehend the greatness of the sovereignty of God which they saw revealed no less gloriously in the miraculous survival of the Jewish people despite its state of dependence, weakness, and dispersion among hostile peoples than in Israel's original establishment as an independent nation. It was for this reason that, in the prayers which it composed, the Assembly restored to the liturgy of its brethren the characterization of God as האל הגדול הגבור והנורא. This designation for God was first used by Moses (Deut. 10:17). Later, however, Jeremiah and Daniel had deleted the adjectives *gibor* and *nora* in view of the tragic era of national disaster that had befallen our people. Eventually, the Men of the Great Assembly restored them; as the Sages put it, (ibid.) החזירו העטרה ליושנה "they restored the crown of glorification to its former splendor." They were convinced that all the centuries of *Galuth* that were to come would be no less significant in our history than their own era, that of the Second Temple, which they felt was merely an introductory period to what was to follow. They manifested this conviction by composing prayers and establishing that order of worship which have served to this day constantly to improve, enrich and strengthen our spiritual and emotional life with the treasures of the truths of Judaism. But beyond that they gave practical expression to their thinking in the manner in which they accomplished the task which had fallen to them to provide for the continued study and observance of the Law. The precepts and the institutions which they established have prompted and preserved the study and the observance of the Law to this very day. It is in this passage that they set down the three principles which guided them in their own successful endeavors and which they recommended to their successors for adoption.

ב שִׁמְעוֹן הַצַּדִּיק הָיָה מִשְּׁיָרֵי כְנֶסֶת הַגְּדוֹלָה · הוּא הָיָה אוֹמֵר,
עַל־שְׁלֹשָׁה דְבָרִים הָעוֹלָם עוֹמֵד עַל הַתּוֹרָה וְעַל הָעֲבוֹדָה וְעַל
גְּמִילוּת חֲסָדִים:

הוו מתונים בדין. We believe that the term *din* does not only refer to judgments in the narrower meaning of property rights, *dinei memonoth* and *dinei nefashoth*, but also includes all those decisions that deal with the application of law, such as דן את הדין, זיכה את החייב וכו׳, טימא את הטהור וכו׳, דן את הדין, זיכה וחייב, טימא וטיהר, אסר והתיר (Bechoroth 28b, Chullin 44b); in these passages the term *dan eth hadin* seems to connote the general, and the passages *zika* etc. which follow apparently denote the particulars under these headings. הוו מתונים בדין is an admonition counseling the expounder of the Law and the judge to consider each case on its own merits and from every possible angle and not to render decisions in routine fashion.

העמידו תלמידים הרבה The Torah is *"morasha kehilath Yaakov"*; it is meant to be the common possession of the entire community, and the maximum dissemination of the knowledge of the Law is viewed as our supreme task and our most sacred concern. The prayerful wish מי יתן כל עם ה׳ נביאים was not an idle phrase in the mouth of Moses; it spelled out what he and his loyal successors viewed as their supreme task in life. In this way every Jew was to be rendered capable of consulting the original sources of the Law by himself to find guidance for his daily life. At the same time, this means that the decisions handed down by the judges and by the expounders of the Law would be subject to control by the largest possible number among the general Jewish public. In all likelihood the sages of Jewish religious doctrine are now and have always been the only teachers in any religion on earth to regard it as the supreme goal of their endeavors to render their own services superfluous.

ועשו סיג לתורה. Keep ושמרתם את משמרתי (Lev. 18:30) עשו משמרת למשמרתי the charge which I have placed into your keeping; make provisions to guard the Law against transgression and to promote its observance. This task had been entrusted to the authorities of the Law from the very outset, when the Law was given; as a matter of fact we have *takanoth* and *gezeroth*, provisions and precepts to promote and preserve the observance of the Law, that date back to Moses and King Solomon. Likewise, the wording of the law: לא תסור מן הדבר אשר יגידו לך ימין ושמאל (Deut. 17:11) imposes upon us the obligation not to deviate, either to the right or to the left, from any ordinances that may be enacted by future expounders of the Torah. However, despite the fact that, according to the Law, these authorities actually had the power to declare as universally binding any provision they might make to safeguard the observance of the Law, they did not, as a rule, make use of these broad powers but

2.   Shimon the Just was one of the last survivors of the Great Assembly. He used to say: The world is based on three things; the Torah, Serving God and active loving-kindness.

---

endowed their provisions with full legal force only once these enactments had received a final stamp of approval in the form of acceptance, in practice, by a majority of the people פשט איסורו ברוב ישראה גזרו וקבלו (*Avod. Zar. 36*). It is quite clear, of course, that maximum dissemination of the knowledge of the Law could act as a powerful agent to predispose the people for the acceptance and observance of such enactments. Moreover, such maximum dissemination and preservation of Torah knowledge, as well as the provisions designed to safeguard observance, were of commanding importance particularly in those times which the Men of the Great Assembly in their wisdom foresaw as eras of increasing dispersion when the people would be moved physically further and further away from the spiritual center of the nation where teaching and guidance could be obtained and at the same time where they would be exposed to an infinite number of temptations to deviate from the path of scrupulous observance.

2.   At the end of this Chapter there is a verse reading על שלשה דברים העולם קים. The difference in meaning between the term *omed* as used in this verse and *kayam*, in Mishna 18 seems to be as follows: *omed*, lit. "stands": that on which something "stands" or "is based" constitutes its foundation; if it loses that base or foundation it will fall. *Kayam*, on the other hand, denotes a "standing up" or "enduring" through time; i.e. stability or permanence. If a thing loses that on which it depends for stability or permanence it may continue to exist but it will not endure. תורה implies the *knowledge* of the *truth* and the *will of God* with regard to every aspect of our lives, personal and public, individual and social. עבודה denotes *dutiful obedience*, serving God by fulfilling His will in every phase of our lives, personal and public, individual and social. גמילות חסדים signifies selfless, active loving-kindness to promote the welfare of our fellow-men. These are the three things which shape and perfect the world of man and all that pertains to it in accordance with the measure and way of its destiny. Whenever and wherever any of these three are inadequate or altogether lacking there is a gap which cannot be filled and there is no manifest destiny. Without *Torah* the human spirit lacks the wellsprings of true knowledge; it will be blind to that basic, indispensable element which makes man a human being and it will be receptive to everything except truth and right. Without *Avodah* man cannot have the proper attitude toward God, his Master and Creaor, and toward the world into which God put him in order to develop and protect it in accordance with God's will. Instead of serving God he will think he is the master when, as a matter of fact, he will be the slave of his passions and his lust. He will pander to anything that he feels can serve or prejudice his interests, and instead of being exalted

ג אַנְטִיגְנוֹס אִישׁ סוֹכוֹ קִבֵּל מִשִּׁמְעוֹן הַצַּדִּיק · הוּא הָיָה אוֹמֵר,
אַל־תִּהְיוּ כַּעֲבָדִים הַמְשַׁמְּשִׁין אֶת־הָרַב עַל־מְנָת לְקַבֵּל פְּרָס,
אֶלָּא הֱווּ כַּעֲבָדִים הַמְשַׁמְּשִׁין אֶת־הָרַב שֶׁלֹּא עַל־מְנָת לְקַבֵּל
פְּרָס וִיהִי מוֹרָא שָׁמַיִם עֲלֵיכֶם:

ד יוֹסֵי בֶּן־יוֹעֶזֶר אִישׁ צְרֵדָה וְיוֹסֵי בֶּן־יוֹחָנָן אִישׁ יְרוּשָׁלַיִם קִבְּלוּ
מֵהֶם · יוֹסֵי בֶּן־יוֹעֶזֶר אִישׁ צְרֵדָה אוֹמֵר, יְהִי בֵיתְךָ בֵּית וַעַד
לַחֲכָמִים וֶהֱוֵי מִתְאַבֵּק בַּעֲפַר רַגְלֵיהֶם וֶהֱוֵי שׁוֹתֶה בַצָּמָא אֶת־
דִּבְרֵיהֶם:

---

and ennobled by him in accordance with God's purpose, everything he touches
will receive the impress of his depravity and error. If he omits *Gemiluth
Chasadim* he will be without that characteristic which is the very first trait
of godliness. Instead of being God-like in acting as a creator of happiness and
prosperity for his fellow-men, he will harden his heart in callous selfishness,
and mankind will lack that bond of brotherhood and loving-kindness within
which alone all happiness and joy of life can prosper. *Torah* enables man to
do justice to himself; by way of *Avodah* he will meet the requirements of
God; and through *Gemiluth Chasadim* he performs his duty toward his fellow-
men. In all likelihood this is the reason why *Gemiluth Chasadim* is enumerated
as a separate concept even though, in fact, it is also part of *Avodah*, which
is practical, active obedience in the service of God.

3. In Mishna 1 we read that Moses *mesoroh*, "handed down" the Law to
Joshua from whom it passed to the Elders, then from the Elders to the
Prophets and eventually from the Prophets to the Men of the Great Assembly.
In each instance we are told that the Law was "handed down" (or "handed
over") as a precious heritage to be preserved. In each instance the receivers
had become the guardians of the Law by explicit appointment of their elders.
As distinguished from these, Antigonus and all those who followed him were
just members of a group of disciples who studied at the feet of the masters and
"received" the Oral Tradition verbally as they listened to the learned discourses. Since they were acknowledged to be the most capable and proficient
scholars in the group, these men were eventually chosen not by their elders
but by their contemporaries to be teachers and leaders of the nation after the
elders had passed on.

המשמשין: While an *eved* as such does not necessarily have personal contact with his employer, the term *shamash*, like the Hebrew *sharat*, implies

3.   Antigonus of Socho received [the tradition] from Shimon the Just. He used to say: Be not like servants who minister to their master for the sake of receiving a reward, but be like servants who minister to their master not for the sake of a reward, and let the fear of Heaven be upon you.

4.   Yosé ben Yo'ezer of Tzeredah and Yosé ben Yochanan of Jerusalem received [the tradition] from them. Yosé ben Yo'ezer of Tzeredah says: Let your house be a meeting place for sages, cover yourself with the dust of their feet and drink in their words thirstily.

---

personal ministrations to a master. It can be readily presumed that there do exist *avadim* who, if they have the good fortune to be called upon to render personal services to their employer, derive so much pleasure from this personal contact with their master that they regard it sufficient reward in itself and have no thought of any other compensation. Such, Antigonus declares, should be our relationship with God in our life's service to Him. The fulfillment of His commandments should not be treated as an activity apart or remote from Him. Rather, every commandment should serve to call us into His presence, before His countenance, in order to perform, within His sight, a service pleasing to Him. Every such act should bring us nearer to Him and should so enrich us with His approval that the realization of His nearness and approval may render the true human being so happy that he will find his "service to God" to be his richest reward and it will not even occur to him to seek additional compensation. This is that attitude which our Sages characterize elsewhere by the terms לשמה ,לשם שמים.

ויהי מורא שמים עליכם. In human relationships, the greater intimacy of contact involved in personal ministrations to a master usually tends to lessen the servant's respect for his employer. But the Lord says, (Lev. 10:3) בקרבי אקדש: The nearer a man is to Me, the more do I expect to be sanctified by him, so that My nearness may preserve him from even the slightest transgression; hence the passage משמשין שלא על מנת לקבל פרס is followed by the admonition ויהי מורא שמים עליכם.

4.   ביתך. Be such a friend to learning and show such kindness and hospitality to its guardians and teachers that they will feel drawn to your home and will be happy to gather there. Accord them a place of honor in your house, sit at their feet and listen intently to their conversation, for, as the Sages state elsewhere אפילו שיחת חולין של תלמידי חכמים צריכה למוד (Succah 21b): Even the ordinary conversation of sages [is instructive and] should be studied.

ה יוֹסֵי בֶּן־יוֹחָנָן אִישׁ יְרוּשָׁלַיִם אוֹמֵר, יְהִי בֵיתְךָ פָּתוּחַ לָרְוָחָה
וְיִהְיוּ עֲנִיִּים בְּנֵי בֵיתֶךָ, וְאַל־תַּרְבֶּה שִׂיחָה עִם הָאִשָּׁה, בְּאִשְׁתּוֹ
אָמְרוּ קַל וָחֹמֶר בְּאֵשֶׁת חֲבֵרוֹ· מִכַּאן אָמְרוּ חֲכָמִים כָּל־הַמַּרְבֶּה
שִׂיחָה עִם הָאִשָּׁה גּוֹרֵם רָעָה לְעַצְמוֹ וּבוֹטֵל מִדִּבְרֵי תוֹרָה וְסוֹפוֹ
יוֹרֵשׁ גֵּיהִנֹּם :

י יְהוֹשֻׁעַ בֶּן־פְּרַחְיָה וְנִתַּאי הָאַרְבֵּלִי קִבְּלוּ מֵהֶם· יְהוֹשֻׁעַ בֶּן־פְּרַחְיָה
אוֹמֵר, עֲשֵׂה לְךָ רַב וּקְנֵה לְךָ חָבֵר וֶהֱוֵי דָן אֶת־כָּל־הָאָדָם
לְכַף זְכוּת :

---

5. לרוחה. In Exod. 8:11 the term *revacha* is used to denote "relief", literally
a "widening" or "loosening" of the bonds of want and distress. Said Rabbi
Yosé: Let your home be open always to those who suffer and seek relief, and
even if you are not able to eliminate all want and distress, be ready at all
all times to ease and relieve suffering to the best of your ability. Let the
poor be members of your household; regard them as children in your home.
Consider your house as established not only for yourself and your immediate
family; let the homeless poor share in the pleasures of your home whenever
and to whatever extent you can, and when you extend your hospitality to the
poor, treat them as you do the members of your own household.

אל תרבה שיחה עם האשה, "Do not או תרבה דברים or אל תדבר הרבה. We are not told
talk too much with your wife." As a matter of fact, the sayings of the Sages are
replete with maxims stressing the high esteem in which womanhood should
be held, the respect and honor due one's wife and particularly the great importance that a husband should attach to the views, opinions and counsel of
his wife. And especially in this context, where we have just read about the
virtues of helpfulness, charity, kindness and hospitality which should emanate
from the home and hence are so greatly dependent on the work and coop-
eration of the wife, the statement immediately following certainly should not
be construed in a way derogatory to her. In fact, this very statement may
well be founded on genuine appreciation of the vital role played by both
husband and wife in the discharge of the task to be fulfilled by the home.
Sichah does not mean serious conversation but merely idle talk and gossip.
Cf. *sichat yeladim* (3:14) and *mi'ut sichah* (6:6). A man who truly respects
his wife will have more to offer her than just trivial talk and idle chatter
for her amusement. He will want to discuss with her the serious concerns of
life and will derive enjoyment from the resulting exchange of views and
counsel. Moreover, engaging in trifling talk with other women and other

5.   Yosé ben Yochanan of Jerusalem says: Let your house be open for relief and let the poor be members of your household. Do not engage in too much idle talk with women. This has been said even with regard to one's own wife; how much more does it apply to the wife of one's neighbor. Accordingly, the Sages said: He who engages in too much idle talk with women brings trouble upon himself; he neglects the study of the Torah and will in the end inherit *Gehinnom*.
6.   Yehoshua ben Perachyah and Nittai the Arbelite received [the tradition] from them. Yehoshua ben Perachyah says: Provide yourself with a teacher, get yourself a companion and judge all men favorably.

---

men's wives may imperil moral purity. מכאן : From these passages was derived this maxim, according to which indulgence in more idle chatter than is seemly even within one's own household may gravely jeopardize the spirit of earnest duty and study to which life should be consecrated.

The tenet of Antigonus is meant to promote *Avodah,* that of Yosé of Tzeredah is aimed at the cultivation of *Torah* and that of Yosé of Jerusalem at the promotion of *Gemiluth Chasadim.* We may well look with admiring envy upon a society in which it is expected even of ordinary citizens to make their homes the dwelling places of learning (see Mishna 4) and of active loving-kindness (Mishna 5).

6.   The injunction עשה לך רב corresponds to *Torah;* וקנה לך חבר to *Avodah* and הוי דן וכו' to *Gemiluth Chasadim.* "Provide yourself" with a teacher; bring it to pass that a capable man accepts you as his disciple and thus affords you an opportunity to attain spiritual perfection through his wisdom and knowledge. We are not told to "get" ourselves a teacher, for in accordance with Judaism, the Torah, and particularly the תורה שבעל פה, the Talmud, should be taught without financial reward; indeed, it is a *mitzvah* incumbent on everyone to impart to qualified disciples whatever teachings of God one may have acquired. A *chaver,* a friend and companion in life, on the other hand, who is a helper and counselor at our side in our work and our endeavors must be "got" or "acquired"; this means that we must win him by way of accommodation, association and empathy; hence we are told קנה לך חבר. "Teacher" and "friend"—these appelations represent the highest level on which we can cherish another human being and as a rule there are only a few whom we are able to designate as such. But even if there are only a few people chosen for and by us to whom we can feel so close and who will feel so close to us in return, we must be careful not to be too harsh in our judgment of others and certainly we must not be so arrogant as to seek to keep aloof from them. Rather, it should be our endeavor to keep the best possible opinion of all men, and even in instances where their conduct seems to us of dubious and questionable character, we should be as charitable as we can in our judgment of them.

ז נִתַּאי הָאַרְבֵּלִי אוֹמֵר הַרְחֵק מִשָּׁכֵן רָע וְאַל־תִּתְחַבֵּר לָרָשָׁע
וְאַל־תִּתְיָאֵשׁ מִן־הַפּוּרְעָנוּת:

ח יְהוּדָה בֶן טַבַּאי וְשִׁמְעוֹן בֶּן שָׁטַח קִבְּלוּ מֵהֶם · יְהוּדָה בֶן־טַבַּאי
אוֹמֵר, אַל־תַּעַשׂ עַצְמְךָ כְּעוֹרְכֵי הַדַּיָּנִין וּכְשֶׁיִּהְיוּ בַּעֲלֵי הַדִּין
עוֹמְדִים לְפָנֶיךָ יִהְיוּ בְעֵינֶיךָ כִּרְשָׁעִים וּכְשֶׁנִּפְטָרִים מִלְּפָנֶיךָ יִהְיוּ
בְעֵינֶיךָ כְּזַכָּאִין כְּשֶׁקִּבְּלוּ עֲלֵיהֶם אֶת־הַדִּין:

ט שִׁמְעוֹן בֶּן־שָׁטַח אוֹמֵר, הֱוֵי מַרְבֶּה לַחֲקוֹר אֶת־הָעֵדִים
וֶהֱוֵי זָהִיר בִּדְבָרֶיךָ שֶׁמָּא מִתּוֹכָם יִלְמְדוּ לְשַׁקֵּר:

י שְׁמַעְיָה וְאַבְטַלְיוֹן קִבְּלוּ מֵהֶם · שְׁמַעְיָה אוֹמֵר, אֱהַב אֶת־
הַמְּלָאכָה וּשְׂנָא אֶת־הָרַבָּנוּת וְאַל־תִּתְוַדַּע לָרָשׁוּת:

---

7. We can remove ourselves physically, by changing our residence, from a
neighbor who could have a harmful and detrimental effect on us by reason
of his quarrelsome, underhanded character and downright wickedness. Therefore we are told רע משכן הרחק. In or daily dealings with others, however, we
cannot avoid contact with individuals who have thrown God's Law aside.
But we neither need nor should enter into close relations with them. "Do
not associate with them," do not make common cause with them and particularly—and this is the literal meaning of *hithchaber le*— do not become
a member in communities in which *reshaim* dominate. In the end there is a
penalty to pay for all these things, for remaining near an evil neighbor as
well as for association with evil men. Even if you have maintained such
associations over a long period of time without feeling any adverse effects,
it is inevitable that your thoughtlessness and indifference must result in harm
to you in the long run.

8. Should you be called upon to function as a judge, do not be like the
legal advisors who offer to place their juridicial knowledge at the service of
the litigating parties. Do not instruct them how to testify and how to counter
arguments in court. In your office of judge you must remain silent and abstain from interference in the arguments brought before you. Do not by even
so much as a gesture seek to influence either prosecution or defense. (As distinct from this injunction we have a legal maxim לאלם פיך פתח in Gittin 37b,
Kethuvoth 36a, Choshen Mishpat 17:9, according to which, in extraordinary
cases only, of course, it is the right and at times even the duty of the judge
to call attention to or elaborate upon particulars that were not stressed in

7. Nittai the Arbelite says: Keep away from an evil neighbor and do not associate with a lawless man, and do not give up the belief in retribution.

8. Yehudah ben Tabbai and Shimon ben Shetach received [the tradition] from them. Yehudah ben Tabbai says: In the office of judge, do not act the counsel, and as long as the parties [in the lawsuit] stand before you, let them be as guilty in your eyes, but when they depart from you, once they have submitted to the judgment, regard them [both] as innocent.

9. Shimon ben Shetach says: Examine the witnesses thoroughly and be careful with your words lest they learn through them to falsify.

10. Shemayah and Avtalyon received [the tradition] from them. Shemayah says: Love work, hate the holding of high office and do not seek to become intimate with the authorities.

---

the evidence due to obvious ignorance or awkwardness on the part of one of the litigating parties.). וכשיהיו וכו׳, As long as the parties are before you, you must view them both as equally unreliable and must interpret and evaluate their allegations objectively, dispassionately, without regard to personalities, and solely on the merit of their testimony. For there are disputes in which even the best man may be in the wrong and the worst man in the right. On the other hand, once the parties have accepted your judgment and the case has been closed, do not carry with you into your life outside of court any adverse impression you may have obtained, without realizing it, of one or the other party during the hearing. Once their dispute has been settled you must regard them both as equally free of guilt.

9. חקירה The purpose of the examination and questioning of witnesses is, by probing into the particulars in the case, to uncover inconsistencies between the testimonies of two or more of the witnesses. In this process, unguarded statements or ill-considered phrasing of questions on the part of the judge can easily reveal to the witnesses the sort of testimony that may be beneficial or detrimental to either side and cause them to deviate from the truth.

10. It seems that the purpose of these three maxims of Shemayah is to counsel us to preserve our personal independence. We are told: Love work, for it is your assurance of economic independence. Hate the holding of high office, for the office-holder quickly becomes a slave to his position. He will do things—or he will believe that, for the sake of his position, he must do certain things—which actually are contrary to his own views and inclinations and which he would never do if he were free to follow his own principles and his personal philosophies of life. Finally, do not seek to become intimate with the ruling authorities; for this is the literal meaning of רשות. Such relationships may impair your independence and may make you do many

יא אַבְטַלְיוֹן אוֹמֵר, חֲכָמִים הִזָּהֲרוּ בְּדִבְרֵיכֶם שֶׁמָּא תָחוּבוּ חוֹבַת גָּלוּת וְתִגְלוּ לִמְקוֹם מַיִם הָרָעִים וְיִשְׁתּוּ הַתַּלְמִידִים הַבָּאִים אַחֲרֵיכֶם וְיָמוּתוּ וְנִמְצָא שֵׁם שָׁמַיִם מִתְחַלֵּל:

יב הִלֵּל וְשַׁמַּאי קִבְּלוּ מֵהֶם · הִלֵּל אוֹמֵר, הֱוֵי מִתַּלְמִידָיו שֶׁל־אַהֲרֹן אוֹהֵב שָׁלוֹם וְרוֹדֵף שָׁלוֹם אוֹהֵב אֶת־הַבְּרִיּוֹת וּמְקָרְבָן לַתּוֹרָה:

יג הוּא הָיָה אוֹמֵר, נְגִיד שְׁמָא אֲבַד שְׁמֵהּ וּדְלָא מוֹסִיף יָסֵף וּדְלָא יַלִּיף קְטָלָא חַיָּב וּדְאִשְׁתַּמַּשׁ בְּתָגָא חֲלָף:

---

things that may coincide with the will, the inclinations, wishes and views of your powerful friends whom you do not want to alienate but that may be quite contrary to your own wishes, views and inclinations. Only one who is content to live unobtrusively, to remain in a humble position and to sustain himself by dint of his own labors can be truly free.

11. According to the Torah the penalty for accidental manslaughter was *Galuth,* exile in the form of enforced relocation to one of the Cities of Refuge. In this Mishna the "penalty of *Galuth*" is used with reference also to moral manslaughter, Scholars are warned against making rash or careless statements in their discourses that might cause the moral downfall of their disciples. They are cautioned against delivering themselves of utterances that are inaccurate, vague or ambiguous and that may inspire erroneous views and result in spiritual and moral deviations from goodness and truth. A pernicious process of this type, started by a learned discourse, is portrayed here in allegoric terms as follows: The lecturer "comes upon a place of perilous waters," meaning that he presents to his audience teachings and views which may endanger moral life if they are misinterpreted, without cautioning his listeners against such misinterpretation. As a result, his disciples will follow the material presented in the lecture; they will accept the erroneous interpretation as if it were taught by their master and thereby they will fall victim to moral disintegration. Such an error on the part of a lecturer is also referred to by the Hebrew term *galah.* He "departs" or "emigrates" from the sheltered abode of truth and strays into perilous places which it would have been better had they remained unknown to him. Or perhaps תגלו is derived not from *galah* but from its homonym, *galah* meaning "to uncover". For in the *Kal* inflection, too, *galah* means "to uncover". In this case, the interpretation would be that the lecturer "uncovers" wells of poisoned water and leaves them exposed instead of re-covering them with a lid to protect the passer-by.

11.   Avtalyon says: Scholars, be careful with your words, for you may incur the penalty of *Galuth* and come upon a place of evil waters, and the disciples who follow you may drink from them and die, and the Name of Heaven would be profaned.

12.   Hillel and Shammai received [the tradition] from them. Hillel says: Be of the disciples of Aaron, loving peace and pursuing peace, loving [your fellow] creatures and bringing them nearer to the Torah.

13.   He used to say: He who seeks a name loses his name; he who does not increase [his knowledge] decreases [it]; he who does not study is deserving of death he who makes [improper] use of the crown [of the Torah] will pass away.

---

12.   In the Book of Malachi (2:6) it is said of Aaron that בשלום ובמישור הלך אתי ורבים השיב מעון "He walked with Me in peace and uprightness and brought many back from sin", a description to which the characterization given in this Mishna corresponds. רודף שלום is more than אוהב שלום The "lover of peace" merely avoids whatever may endanger peace, but the *rodef shalom* actively does whatever he can to restore peace that has already fled, and will be ready to make whatever sacrifice he can for the sake of peace except that, of course, he must not under any circumstances compromise the loyalty he owes to God and to his duty.

בריות, lit. "creatures" is a term embracing all of mankind without distinction. He loves all men because they are the creatures of God.

13.   A good name that endures must come unsought; it will come only to him who performs good and commendable deeds and acts of helpfulness for no other motive but out of his sense of duty without caring what others may think. As for him who is greedy for honor and fame, who is motivated in his actions solely by the ambition to acquire a name for himself, his fellow-men will soon discover that he is prompted by selfish motives alone. Besides, his gluttony for fame and honors will quickly lead him also to reprehensible conduct, and then whatever good reputation he may have gained at the outset will vanish apace. There is, however, one field in which no one should ever feel that he has done enough, and that is study and practical observance. He who stands still in these paths is actually regressing. He who does not study is not worthy of life because he neglects to acquaint himself with the tasks for which he was given life and to acquire the skills and knowledge necessary for their fulfillment. This statement seems harsh but it was never more justified than it was in those past days in the history of our people when all schooling was free of charge and everyone possessed of knowledge deemed it his duty to give freely of his wisdom to anyone seeking it. Certainly there has never been one more fully within his rights to make such a statement than was Hillel. According to the account in Yoma 35b, Hillel was

יד הוּא הָיָה אוֹמֵר, אִם אֵין אֲנִי לִי מִי לִי וּכְשֶׁאֲנִי לְעַצְמִי מָה
אֲנִי וְאִם לֹא עַכְשָׁו אֵימָתַי:

טו שַׁמַּאי אוֹמֵר, עֲשֵׂה תוֹרָתְךָ קֶבַע אֱמוֹר מְעַט וַעֲשֵׂה הַרְבֵּה
וֶהֱוֵי מְקַבֵּל אֶת־כָּל־הָאָדָם בְּסֵבֶר פָּנִים יָפוֹת:

טז רַבָּן גַּמְלִיאֵל אוֹמֵר, עֲשֵׂה לְךָ רַב וְהִסְתַּלֵּק מִן הַסָּפֵק וְאַל־
תַּרְבֶּה לְעַשֵּׂר אֲמָדוֹת:

---

so poor in his youth that he earned no more than one *tarpek* a day by his
labors. Of this he had to give half to the doorkeeper of the House of Study
as an admission fee; the other half had to do for his wants and the needs
of his family. It came to pass one day that he could find no work and hence
could not pay the doorkeeper. Therefore he lay down atop the skylight on
the roof of the House of Study and from that position he listened to the
learned discourses of Shemayah and Abtalyon, his teachers, all night long.
The next morning it still seemed to be unusually dark in the House of Study.
When some men investigated the cause, they came upon Hillel buried under
a foot of snow that had fallen during the night. Therefore it is said הלל מחייב
עניים. If a man pleads poverty and economic worries as an excuse for not
studying, let him be reminded of the example set by Hillel.

ודאשתמש בתגא: תגא, "the crown", refers to the *Kether Torah,* the crown
of knowledge of the Torah. He who would debase this "crown" to serve as
a common tool for the acquisition of honor or personal advantage, חלף;
he will not acquire either of these on a basis of permanence. This sentence
may be interpreted as a justification for the statement that precedes it. If
no one will exploit his knowledge of the Torah for financial gain and everyone will give instruction without payment, there will be no excuse for anyone
not to study.

14. It is only through his own efforts that a man can attain spiritual fitness
and moral worth, which are the most essential attributes to which he can
aspire. Similarly, it is primarily upon himself, his own diligence, his own
efforts and his own good sense that man must depend in the process of
acquiring and certainly of preserving the worldly goods he needs. True, others
can help him in these endeavors, but without earnest effort on his own part
he will not be able to acquire, much less keep whatever there is to be gained.
But even though he may have become who and what he is solely by dint of
his own efforts, a man must never say: "Since it is solely by my own efforts
that I have become what I am, I will use my attainments for myself alone."
For it is only when, in selfless devotion, he actively works to create, to establish
and to increase the happiness and prosperity of his fellowmen that a man

14. He used to say: If I am nothing to myself, who will be for me? And if I am for myself only, what am I? And if not now, when?

15. Shammai says: Make your study of the Torah a regular activity, promise little but do much, and receive all men with a kindly countenance.

16. Rabban Gamliel says: Provide yourself with a teacher and free yourself of doubt, for you must not give an excess tithe through guesswork.

---

begins to become truly human in the image of his God. If he exists for himself alone, of what value is he? And never put off accomplishing this human calling either for yourself, or, through you, for others, for to this task every moment of your life should be devoted. Do you know whether, indeed, you still will have another moment in which to do the work?

15. The study of Torah is our first and most important task because it determines the extent to which we will understand and fulfill our life's duties. Therefore, regardless of any other pursuit to which we may give of our time, we must not leave the study of the Torah to chance but should establish a regular daily time and schedule for study and adhere to it, for otherwise we might allow other pursuits to keep us from study and as a result we would drift away more and more from this source of our spiritual sustenance. But while we are told to establish a definite schedule for our studies in advance, we must not make the same inflexible plans as regards our actions. When it comes to action, we should promise little but do all the more. However, even though our spoken word should not promise too much or too easily, our conduct and approach to every human being should be so friendly in character that all will be convinced that we are kindly disposed toward them and that we are ready at all times to the best of our abilities to fulfill whatever good and reasonable request another may make of us.

16. It is only through study with a reliable and scrupulous teacher whom you can consult in cases of doubt that you can establish with certainty what your duty is and how you should conduct yourself. Therefore see that you provide yourself with a teacher who has these qualifications. You must not think that you can manage without instruction by simply following the stricter precept in cases of doubt, by refraining from what may even be permissible and by doing more than is actually required of you. To be sure, if you have no possibility to obtain such instruction, you have no other choice but to follow this course. On the other hand, you must not believe that this alternative will safeguard you from error in *every* instance. The illustration given in this Mishna has reference, as an example, to *maaser*, the mandatory tithe of grain. If, instead of measuring out the amount of grain from which the tithe is to be taken, a man takes the tithe by guesswork, he would be remiss in his duty not only if he should thereby make his tithe too little but also if

יי שִׁמְעוֹן בְּנוֹ אוֹמֵר, כָּל־יָמַי גָּדַלְתִּי בֵּין הַחֲכָמִים וְלֹא מָצָאתִי
לַגּוּף טוֹב מִשְּׁתִיקָה וְלֹא הַמִּדְרָשׁ עִקָּר אֶלָּא הַמַּעֲשֶׂה, וְכָל־הַמַּרְבֶּה
דְּבָרִים מֵבִיא חֵטְא:

יח רַבָּן שִׁמְעוֹן בֶּן־גַּמְלִיאֵל אוֹמֵר, עַל־שְׁלֹשָׁה דְּבָרִים הָעוֹלָם
קַיָּם עַל־הָאֱמֶת וְעַל־הַדִּין וְעַל־הַשָּׁלוֹם שֶׁנֶּאֱמַר אֱמֶת וּמִשְׁפַּט
שָׁלוֹם שִׁפְטוּ בְּשַׁעֲרֵיכֶם:

רַבִּי חֲנַנְיָא בֶּן־עֲקַשְׁיָא אוֹמֵר, רָצָה הַקָּדוֹשׁ בָּרוּךְ הוּא לְזַכּוֹת אֶת־יִשְׂרָאֵל
לְפִיכָךְ הִרְבָּה לָהֶם תּוֹרָה וּמִצְוֹת. שֶׁנֶּאֱמַר יְיָ חָפֵץ לְמַעַן צִדְקוֹ יַגְדִּיל תּוֹרָה
וְיַאְדִּיר: קדיש.

---

he should make it too much. For instance, if a man determines his tithe by
taking one out of every five instead of one of ten, the tithe itself would
contain an unredeemed part which would be *tevel* and therefore *assur*.
המרבה במעשרות פירותיו מתוקנים ומעשרותיו מקולקלין (Eruvin 50a).

17. The של"ה interprets this Mishna as follows: I have spent all my time in
the company of sages and from them,who wield their influence through the
spoken word, I have learned the true significance of speech. But as regards
the physical aspects of life and the personal affairs of men, I have found
silence to be the best policy. One is duty-bound to make provision for these
things but one must not talk much about them. Let the speech of men and
their discussions center on spiritual and moral concerns. Indeed, there is
nothing more offensive than the pompous gusto with which men converse
about the merits of food and drink. As a matter of fact, there are limits to
the usefulness of speech even in the teaching and inquiry associated with
things moral and spiritual; deeds and accomplishments count the most. *Too
much* talk is always bad. Clarity and conciseness always are conducive to the
desired ends. Needless effusions of words weaken even the best-taken point
and verbosity invites error and wrong. As the Sages point out, in most of
the "lamentations" that deplore error, the letter *Pe* (mouth) comes before the
letter *Ayin* (eye); the mouth utters what the eye has not seen and the mind

17. Shimon his son says: All my life I have grown up amongst sages and have found nothing better for the physical welfare of man than silence; study is not the most important thing but practice, and too much talk brings sin.

18. Rabban Shimon ben Gamliel said: By virtue of three things does the world endure: truth, justice, and peace, as it is said: You shall administer truth and the justice of peace in your gates.

Rabbi Chananya ben Akashyah said: The Holy One, blessed be He, desired to bestow great favor on Israel; hence He gave them Torah and laws in abundant measure. For it is said: God was pleased for the sake of His righteousness to render the Torah increasingly great and glorious.

---

has not tested. One of the worst consequences of profuse talk, however, is that people who have spoken long and much and zealously of and in behalf of a cause may persuade themselves that this alone constitutes action, and should a voice within them accuse them of being remiss in their concrete efforts for the cause, they will calm their conscience by recalling the enthusiasm and the brilliance with which they had carried on the discussion of the matter at hand!

18. If *truth* should be removed from human speech and understanding so that truth could no longer be known, uttered and taught, and speech would serve man only to conceal his thoughts and to spread error, falsehood and deceit; if *justice* should be eliminated from the deeds and the affairs of men so that men would no longer honor right as the most sacred of inalienable values before which all selfishness, violence and personal interest must bow and there would be no supreme authority to defend the rights of all with steadfast determination and against every act of aggression and usurpation; if *peace* should be banished from the sentiments and the esteem of men so that there would be no one who of his own free will would waive for the sake of peace whatever is his to sacrifice—save, of course, his conscience and his duty; if truth and justice and peace should vanish from the earth; then, no matter what else the world might have in which to glory, the affairs of men will attain neither stability nor permanent value.

כל ישראל וכו׳

א רַבִּי אוֹמֵר, אֵיזוֹ הִיא דֶרֶךְ יְשָׁרָה שֶׁיָבוֹר לוֹ הָאָדָם כָּל־שֶׁהִיא תִפְאֶרֶת לְעשֶׂהָ וְתִפְאֶרֶת לוֹ מִן הָאָדָם, וֶהֱוֵה זָהִיר בְּמִצְוָה קַלָה כְּבַחֲמוּרָה שֶׁאֵין אַתָּה יוֹדֵעַ מַתַּן שְׂכָרָן שֶׁל־מִצְוֹת, וֶהֱוֵי מְחַשֵׁב הֶפְסֵד מִצְוָה כְּנֶגֶד שְׂכָרָהּ וּשְׂכַר עֲבֵרָה כְּנֶגֶד הֶפְסֵדָהּ · הִסְתַּכֵּל בִּשְׁלֹשָׁה דְבָרִים וְאֵין אַתָּה בָא לִידֵי עֲבֵרָה, דַּע מַה־לְמַעְלָה מִמְךָ עַיִן רוֹאָה וְאֹזֶן שׁוֹמַעַת וְכָל־מַעֲשֶׂיךָ בַּסֵּפֶר נִכְתָּבִים:

---

1. When we are faced with a choice of action, there are two things which we must consider; first, whether the action would be in accord with the will and the ordinances of God so that its performance as such will be to our credit, and secondly, whether there is a chance that it may be misinterpreted by others. This is the same principle that is set forth elsewhere in the command והייתם נקיים מה׳ ומישראל. When it comes to the performance of a Divine commandment, be as careful and as scrupulous in the execution of one which is easy to fulfill, or seems easy to you, as you would be with one that appears more difficult to fulfill, for you do not know the standard by which God apportions the reward for our good deeds. We are here told מתן שכרן, as distinct from שכר מצוה ועברה which follows. For good deeds and sins alike carry a two-fold recompense. First, there is the objective reward or punishment; this comes to us sooner or later, whichever may be ordained in God's decree, either in this world or in the world to come, it is to this form of recompense that מתן שכרן refers. The other recompense is spiritual in character and it comes to us immediately; it is inherent in the good deed or in the sin itself. The immediate reward of any Divine command scrupulously performed is a sense of moral elevation, an increase in our moral strength, and the awareness, most blissful of all, that we are worthy of the nearness of God because we have faithfully carried out our duty toward Him. The recompense for any evil act is also instantaneous; it takes the form of a sense of loss of moral purity, a weakening of moral fiber, a greater propensity to additional sin, and most crushing of all, the realization which renders us unable to look up calmly to our God; namely, that we have failed to fulfill our purpose, sinned against our destiny and hence forfeited the approval of God and, indeed, the right to be satisfied with ourselves. Such reward and such punishment are easy enough to comprehend; it is to these that the terms שכר מצוה and הפסד עברה in this Mishna refer. We are admonished to balance any sacrifice of pleasures and possessions that may be involved in the fulfillment of a Divine command over against the gain, surpassing all else, embodied in the sense of happiness with which faithful perseverance in our duty and its performance fills us.

1. Rabbi [Yehudah Ha-Nasi] said: Which is the right course that a man should choose? Any one which in itself does credit to him who adopts it and which also brings him honor from men; and be careful of a light precept even as of a grave one, for you do not know the reward for the commandments; balance the loss incurred in the performance of a commandment against its reward and the gain gotten from a sin against the loss it entails. Consider three things and you will not fall into the grip of sin. Know what is above you: a seeing eye and a hearing ear, and that all your deeds are recorded in the The Book.

Indeed, the greater the sacrifices we have to make to duty, the greater the happiness inherent in duty done. On the other hand, balance any promise of unlawful gain and impious pleasures by which iniquitous temptation might seek to lure us away from the path of duty over against the irreplaceable loss of inner purity and peace and the persistent, crushing torture inherent in that sense of guilt which compels us to condemn ourselves and to be denied the approval of our God. But then we know of nothing that makes it easier for us gladly to do good and steadfastly to avoid all evil than to keep before us at all times the three things mentioned in this Mishna; namely, the "seeing eye" and the "hearing ear" which are directed upon us from on high, and the fact that all our deeds will be recorded in "The Book". The knowledge that whatever we say and do is seen and heard by a Supreme Being Who rules over us and over all else as well certainly provides us with the most powerful incentive for being both careful [to avoid evil] and joyously ready [to do good] in all our words and actions. However, these attitudes of prudence and willingness are enhanced still further by the knowledge that whatever we do will be recorded בספר in "The Book". It is not *besefer* but *basefer*. As we have noted in our Commentary to Exodus (32:32) all the many phases of the world's development under the guidance of God are regarded as one uniform whole, "one book", as it were, in which there is room to record everything of significance in this process of continuous growth. "Never forget," we are told here, "that the consequences and repercussions of everything you do reach far beyond the fleeting time span in which your act occurred. God is mindful even of the least conspicuous of your actions, and they all will be recalled to you when your life will pass in review at the end of your days; and what is more, they will continue to be operative, for good or for evil, through all the days to come. This should be sufficient reason for you to do nothing of which you might have to be ashamed in the presence of God and of your own self-respect; it should be sufficient reason to be careful, with all your deeds, to plant nothing but seeds of goodness into the soil of the future yet unborn."

ב רַבָּן גַּמְלִיאֵל בְּנוֹ שֶׁל־רַבִּי יְהוּדָה הַנָּשִׂיא אוֹמֵר, יָפֶה תַלְמוּד
תּוֹרָה עִם דֶּרֶךְ אֶרֶץ שֶׁיְּגִיעַת שְׁנֵיהֶם מַשְׁכַּחַת עָוֹן וְכָל־תּוֹרָה
שֶׁאֵין עִמָּהּ מְלָאכָה סוֹפָהּ בְּטֵלָה וְגוֹרֶרֶת עָוֹן וְכָל־הָעוֹסְקִים עִם־
הַצִּבּוּר יִהְיוּ עוֹסְקִים עִמָּהֶם לְשֵׁם שָׁמַיִם שֶׁזְּכוּת אֲבוֹתָם מְסַיַּעְתָּם
וְצִדְקָתָם עוֹמֶדֶת לָעַד וְאַתֶּם מַעֲלֶה אֲנִי עֲלֵיכֶם שָׂכָר הַרְבֵּה
כְּאִלּוּ עֲשִׂיתֶם:

ג הֱווּ זְהִירִין בָּרָשׁוּת שֶׁאֵין מְקָרְבִין לוֹ לְאָדָם אֶלָּא לְצֹרֶךְ

---

2. The term דרך ארץ includes all the situations arising from and dependent
upon the circumstance that the earth is the place where the individual must
live, fulfill his destiny and dwell together with others and that he must utilize
resources and conditions provided on earth in order to live and to accomplish
his purpose. Accordingly, the term *derech eretz* is used primarily to refer to
ways of earning a living, to the social order that prevails on earth, as well
as to the mores and considerations of courtesy and propriety arising from
social living and also to things pertinent to good breeding and general edu-
cation. We believe that the explanation שיגיעת שניהם וכו׳ implies that the term
derech eretz as used here denotes, above all, the business and occupational
activities carried on for purposes of earning a living. We are not told that
שיגיעת שניהם "keeps away sin" but משכחת that it causes sin to be forgotten,
that it "keeps sinful thoughts from arising." By this, we believe, is meant
that only a way of life devoted to the pursuit of study as well as of economic
independence can take up our time to such a degree that there will be no
unoccupied hours during which we could indulge in thoughts that are far
from good and that could make us drift away from the path of goodness.
Nay, more, וכל תורה וכו׳, he who does not pursue some gainful employment
alongside the study of the Torah runs the risk of being forced to stop his
studies because of poverty and of being driven to wrongdoing by destitution
and misery. It is difficult to find the logical connection between the foregoing
statements and the next sentence which begins with the words וכל העוסקים.
We believe that there is a connection as follows: After Rabbi Yehudah Ha-
Nasi, the compiler of the Mishna, died and had been succeeded by his
son, there began in Babylonia an era when academies of Jewish learning
and Jewish communal life were in full flower. At the same time there was a
steady increase in the number of Jewish settlements outside of Palestine. It
was probably this trend that impelled the son of Rabbenu Yehudah Ha-Nasi
to put stress on those elements that are basic to the maintenance and continu-

2. Rabban Gamliel, the son of Rabbi Yehudah Ha-Nasi, said: The study of Torah together with an occupation is an excellent thing, for the pursuit of both of these [together] keeps sinful thoughts from arising, while any study of Torah without some kind of work must fail in the end and is conducive to sin. Let all those who occupy themselves with the [affairs of the] community do so only for the sake of Heaven, for the merit of their fathers will sustain them and their devotion to duty, too, will endure forever. "But as for you," [says God,] I credit you with great reward, as if you had accomplished it."

3. Be cautious with the ruling authorities, for they befriend a man

---

ation of our existence both as individuals and as a people. These elements are; דרך ארץ, תורה and מלאכה in the case of the *individual,* and conscientious attention to communal affairs in the case of *communities.* In regard to the latter he tells us that all those who occupy themselves with communal affairs should do so only לשם שמים. לשם שמים is a concept typical of the Jewish philosophy of life. It denotes action prompted solely by a sense of duty, without any ulterior motives. In this manner our attention is directed to the great and eternal role of the *community* in Jewish life. The community embodies that which is truly eternal in Jewry. In every age there still survive in the community the merits and the good deeds of generations past, acting as the foundation on and by means of which the present is built. Likewise, all the good and righteous deeds that are performed by that present generation will live on in the community through the generations to come. ואתם, As for you, who attend honestly and faithfully to the affairs of the community, who know how to inspire the members of the community to care for the institutions which they are duty-bound to maintain, and who, with scrupulous honesty and wisdom, make use, to this end, of the resources that have been entrusted to you for this purpose, you will be given great reward just as if you had done it all with your own resources. For, as the Sages state elsewhere גדול המעשה יותר מן העושה (Bava Bathra 9a) he who inspires and causes others to do good deeds and to fulfill their duty has even greater merit than he who does the same good with his own resources. Such devotion to communal affairs demands far more self-denial and sustained faithfulness and devotion than is required for one individual who happens to possess the needed means to decide to use these resources in behalf of the good cause.

3. If our interpretation of the preceding passage is not in error, it may be assumed that this statement was intended to be a supplement to what was said in Mishna 2 regarding the new challenges our people had to face as they dispersed and settled in increasing numbers in lands where alien rulers held

עַצְמָן נִרְאִין כְּאוֹהֲבִין בִּשְׁעַת הֲנָאָתָן וְאֵין עוֹמְדִין לוֹ לְאָדָם בִּשְׁעַת דָּחֳקוֹ:

ד הוּא הָיָה אוֹמֵר, עֲשֵׂה רְצוֹנוֹ כִרְצוֹנֶךָ כְּדֵי שֶׁיַּעֲשֶׂה רְצוֹנְךָ כִרְצוֹנוֹ· בַּטֵּל רְצוֹנְךָ מִפְּנֵי רְצוֹנוֹ כְּדֵי שֶׁיְּבַטֵּל רְצוֹן אֲחֵרִים מִפְּנֵי רְצוֹנֶךָ:

ה הִלֵּל אוֹמֵר, אַל־תִּפְרוֹשׁ מִן־הַצִּבּוּר וְאַל־תַּאֲמִין בְּעַצְמְךָ עַד יוֹם מוֹתְךָ וְאַל־תָּדִין אֶת־חֲבֵרְךָ עַד שֶׁתַּגִּיעַ לִמְקוֹמוֹ וְאַל־תֹּאמַר דָּבָר שֶׁאִי אֶפְשָׁר לִשְׁמוֹעַ שֶׁסּוֹפוֹ לְהִשָּׁמֵעַ וְאַל־תֹּאמַר לִכְשֶׁאֶפָּנֶה אֶשְׁנֶה שֶׁמָּא לֹא תִפָּנֶה:

---

sway. רשות is almost synonymous with רשות "permission", "power", and hence denotes any "authority" in whom power is vested.

4. With these words we are asked to identify our will entirely with the will of God, so that we may perform joyously and willingly whatever is pleasing to God as being fully in accord with our own wishes, and give no place in our aspirations to any endeavor that is not in accordance with the will of God. If we ourselves have no other wishes but those identical with the wishes of God Himself, we will have a greater right than anyone else to hope that our own wishes will be fulfilled and we will have less cause than others to fear such wishes as may be inimical to our welfare.

5. It is not to the individual, but to the community, מורשה קהלת יעקב, that God entrusted His Torah as an inheritance for all the generations to come. For this reason every individual is duty-bound to join forces with his community in thought, in word and in deed and loyally to share in its tasks and obligations, so long as that community proves to be a faithful guardian and supporter of the Torah. Indeed, it is essential in the discharge of his own life's task that the individual be part of a larger community. For whatever he may be able to do on his own is inadequate and short-lived; it is only in conjunction with the achievements of others that his own actions can have importance. Moreover, his good principles and convictions will gain considerable strength and support from the fact that he holds them in common with the whole of a genuinely Jewish community. Let no one, Hillel hastens to add, be so presumptuous as to believe that he is morally perfect and therefore think that he will never need the support of a community to guard him against weakness and error, for man is not immune to error and moral frailty as long as he breathes on earth. Likewise, let no one presume to pass judgment on

only for their own interests; they appear as friends when it is to their advantage but they do not stand by a man in times of distress.

4. He used to say: Do His will as you would do your own will, so that He may do your will just as He does His will. Set aside your will for the sake of His will, so that He may set aside the will of others before your will.

5. Hillel said: Do not set yourself apart from the community; do not be sure of yourself until the day of your death. Do not judge your fellow man until you have been in his position; do not say of any word that it cannot possibly be heard, for in the end it will be heard. And do not say: "When I shall have leisure I shall study" for you may never have leisure.

---

others, for does he know the circumstances of his erring brother and the temptations that led him astray, and how can he know whether, in similar circumstances and exposed to the same temptations, he would have been more steadfast in his devotion to duty?

ואל תאמר. This sentence has been the object of many different interpretations. In our opinion it should be understood in association with the statement preceding it. Accordingly, we would submit the following interpretation. Hillel said: Even if you should be the only person in your community to hold a given view, do not say that you will never be able to gain a hearing from the other members of the community. As long as the view you represent is truly right and aims only at what is good and true, do not refrain from expressing it. Continue your fight, tirelessly and undaunted, for what is good and right, for years, if need be; in the end—provided, of course, that you have fought for your cause solely for its own sake, without ulterior, selfish motives—you will be heard.

And even as you must always maintain close ties with your community, so, too, you must remain in constant touch with the study of the Torah, that source of all truth for individual and community alike. However great the pressures of your other affairs may be, you must set aside a definite period each day for study, as has already been indicated previously, and never postpone your study for a period of leisure that seems more convenient. For it may be that you will never have leisure time "more convenient" for study, and as a result you will drift further and further away from the one source at which you may enrich and set aright your knowledge and your attitude as regards what is good and true.

י הוּא הָיָה אוֹמֵר, אֵין בּוּר יְרֵא חֵטְא וְלֹא עַם הָאָרֶץ חָסִיד
וְלֹא הַבַּיְשָׁן לָמֵד וְלֹא הַקַּפְּדָן מְלַמֵּד וְלֹא כָל־הַמַּרְבֶּה בִסְחוֹרָה
מַחְכִּים וּבַמָּקוֹם שֶׁאֵין אֲנָשִׁים הִשְׁתַּדֵּל לִהְיוֹת אִישׁ:

ז אַף הוּא רָאָה גֻּלְגֹּלֶת אַחַת שֶׁצָּפָה עַל־פְּנֵי הַמָּיִם· אָמַר לָהּ,
עַל דַּאֲטֵיפְתְּ אַטִיפוּךְ וְסוֹף מְטַיְפַיִךְ יְטוּפוּן:

ח הוּא הָיָה אוֹמֵר, מַרְבֶּה בָשָׂר מַרְבֶּה רִמָּה מַרְבֶּה נְכָסִים
מַרְבֶּה דְאָגָה מַרְבֶּה נָשִׁים מַרְבֶּה כְשָׁפִים מַרְבֶּה שְׁפָחוֹת מַרְבֶּה

6. In the preceding Mishna we were admonished to keep in constant touch
with the Teaching of the Law. By way of continuation we are now told that
ignorance is never the mother of virtue. בור : A man who is totally ignorant
has no idea of the conditions that prevail around him and of the duties which
he must fulfill; he will sin without even being aware that he is doing wrong.
עם הארץ : It is true that one who, through his upbringing and personal experience, has come to know the conditions in which he moves and the duties
he must discharge will take care not to do wrong. But if he has received no
instruction in the Teachings of the Law, he cannot be a חסיד. If, as the Sages
are careful to point out, he has not had the benefit of personal association
with, and the personal example of true sages to teach him how properly to
fulfill life's duties in actual practice (this is the type of person to whom the
term *am ha-aretz* refers), he cannot know genuine *chasiduth*, true Jewish
virtuousness. He may attach significance to things which are actually without
value; on the other hand, he may regard as unimportant matters which, in
fact, should be viewed as most significant, and, more often than not, he will
fail to put his pious intentions into proper practice. לא הבישן למד וכו' : He who
is too timid to ask questions for fear of betraying his ignorance to his fellow-
students and will rather go without instruction will never acquire knowledge.
A pedantic person, lacking patience with beginners whose learning capacity is
still largely undeveloped, will not be successful as a teacher. He will frighten
his disciples away and they will learn nothing from him. ובמקום : In circumstances where the affairs of the community receive proper attention and the
good and the right are adequately represented, do not push yourself forward.
Under these conditions modesty is a virtue, and any forwardness on your
part may be presumptuous and may tend to push aside men who are better
qualified than you to do the work. But in situations where true men are
lacking, where the interests of the community suffer for lack of proper leader-

6.   He used to say: An ignorant man cannot be sin-fearing, a man lacking instruction cannot be pious, nor can a timid man learn; a man without patience cannot teach, and one who is too deeply involved in business will not grow in wisdom, and in a place where there are no men, strive to be a man.

7.   Moreover, he saw a skull floating on the surface of the water, and he said to it: Even if they have drowned you because you drowned [others], those who drowned you will themselves be drowned.

8.   He used to say: The more flesh, the more decay; the more property, the more worry; the more women, the more superstition; the more maid-servants, the more lewdness; the more men-servants, the

---

ship, and where, in default of adequate support, goodness and truth remain unrecognized and unrealized—it is your duty to strive to become a man qualified to act as a leader and spokesman, and once you have acquired these skills, endeavor to take part in affairs where articulate leadership is needed, for under such conditions reticence would not be modest but downright criminal.

7.   It was obvious to Hillel that the man whose skull was floating on the water had not died by accident but as the result of violence. The head of a corpse floating on the water will not come off; therefore Hillel had to assume that the person had died by violence, and that the murderers had severed the head from the body and then thrown it into the water. Hence the "drowning of another and being drowned" should be interpreted as an allegory rather than as an actual description of the way in which the murder was committed. (As it is, the literal meaning of אטיף is not "to drown another" but "to wash away" or "to allow to float".) As others, too, have pointed out, it is hardly likely that Hillel's intent had been to postulate that every murder victim must have been a murderer himself and that his murderer will be murdered in turn, for such an assumption would not be borne out by fact. Many an innocent man has been a murder victim and not every murderer dies by the hand of another killer. Rather, the thought Hillel wanted to express must have been as follows: Even though a murder may be, in fact, an execution of a Divinely-ordained death sentence, the murderer is still subject to God's judgment for his crime. "The great Master of the Universe has all things at His service, even folly and crime" (Prov. 26:10).

8.   This is an enumeration of things which may seem eminently desirable to many but which can have an adverse effect on those who possess them. Next, by way of contrast, there are listed a number of values which are all associated with Torah and which bring happiness in direct proportion to the extent to which they are present.

מרבה בשר   refers to obesity resulting from rich foods.

זְמָה מַרְבֶּה עֲבָדִים מַרְבֶּה גָזֵל. מַרְבֶּה תוֹרָה מַרְבֶּה חַיִּים מַרְבֶּה
יְשִׁיבָה מַרְבֶּה חָכְמָה מַרְבֶּה עֵצָה מַרְבֶּה תְבוּנָה מַרְבֶּה צְדָקָה
מַרְבֶּה שָׁלוֹם קָנָה שֵׁם טוֹב קָנָה לְעַצְמוֹ קָנָה לוֹ דִּבְרֵי תוֹרָה
קָנָה לוֹ חַיֵּי הָעוֹלָם הַבָּא:

ט רַבָּן יוֹחָנָן בֶּן־זַכַּאי קִבֵּל מֵהִלֵּל וּמִשַּׁמַּאי· הוּא הָיָה אוֹמֵר, אִם
לָמַדְתָּ תוֹרָה הַרְבֵּה אַל־תַּחֲזִיק טוֹבָה לְעַצְמֶךָ כִּי לְכָךְ נוֹצָרְתָּ:
· חֲמִשָּׁה תַלְמִידִים הָיוּ לוֹ לְרַבָּן יוֹחָנָן בֶּן־זַכַּאי · וְאֵלּוּ הֵן (רַבִּי)
אֱלִיעֶזֶר בֶּן־הוֹרְקְנוֹס (רַבִּי) יְהוֹשֻׁעַ בֶּן־חֲנַנְיָא (רַבִּי) יוֹסֵי הַכֹּהֵן (רַבִּי
שִׁמְעוֹן בֶּן־נְתַנְאֵל (וְרַבִּי) אֶלְעָזָר בֶּן־עֲרָךְ:

יא הוּא הָיָה מוֹנֶה שְׁבָחָם· (רַבִּי) אֱלִיעֶזֶר בֶּן־הוֹרְקְנוֹס בּוֹר סוּד
שֶׁאֵינוֹ מְאַבֵּד טִפָּה (רַבִּי) יְהוֹשֻׁעַ בֶּן־חֲנַנְיָא אַשְׁרֵי יוֹלַדְתּוֹ
(רַבִּי) יוֹסֵי הַכֹּהֵן חָסִיד (רַבִּי) שִׁמְעוֹן בֶּן־נְתַנְאֵל יְרֵא חֵטְא
עֲרָבִי) אֶלְעָזָר בֶּן־עֲרָךְ כְּמַעְיָן הַמִּתְגַּבֵּר:

יב הוּא הָיָה אוֹמֵר, אִם יִהְיוּ כָל־חַכְמֵי יִשְׂרָאֵל בְּכַף
מֹאזְנַיִם וֶאֱלִיעֶזֶר בֶּן־הוֹרְקְנוֹס בְּכַף שְׁנִיָּה מַכְרִיעַ אֶת־כֻּלָּם: אַבָּא
שָׁאוּל אוֹמֵר מִשְּׁמוֹ, אִם יִהְיוּ כָל־חַכְמֵי יִשְׂרָאֵל בְּכַף מֹאזְנַיִם
וֶאֱלִיעֶזֶר בֶּן־הוֹרְקְנוֹס אַף עִמָּהֶם וְאֶלְעָזָר בֶּן־עֲרָךְ בְּכַף שְׁנִיָּה,
מַכְרִיעַ אֶת־כֻּלָּם:

מרבה תורה: The more the Torah will be acquired in theory and observed
in practice, the more will human existence become life in the true, genuine
sense of the word.

מרבה ישיבה may be applicable to teacher and disciple alike, for not only
the disciple but also the teacher will profit in the process of teaching. As he
teaches, the instructor finds that his ideas grow clearer and more logical in
their formulation and expression, and the questions and comments of alert
disciples add to his knowledge. As one of our Sages put it, "It is from my

more larceny; the more Torah, the more life; the more study, the more wisdom; the more counsel, the more understanding; the more devotion to duty, the more peace. One who has acquired a good name has made an acquisition for himself; one who has acquired the words of Torah for himself has acquired Eternal Life for himself.

9.   Rabbi Yochanan ben Zakkai received [the tradition] from Hillel and Shammai. He used to say: If you have learned much Torah, do not pride yourself in it, for this is the purpose for which you were created.

10.   Rabbi Yochanan ben Zakkai had five disciples; namely, Rabbi Eliezer ben Horkenos, Rabbi Yehoshua ben Chananyah, Rabbi Yosé the Priest, Rabbi Shimon ben Nethanel and Rabbi Elazar ben Arach.

11.   He used to enumerate their merits: Rabbi Eliezer ben Horkenos is a whitewashed cistern which loses not a drop. Rabbi Yehoshua ben Chananyah: happy is she who bore him. Rabbi Yosé the Priest is truly pious; Rabbi Shimon ben Nethanel is sin-fearing; Rabbi Elazar ben Arach is like a spring which steadily increases its flow.

12.   He used to say: If all the sages of Israel were in one scale of the balance and Eliezer ben Horkenos in the other, he would outweigh them all. Abba Shaul said in his name: If all the sages of Israel, including Eliezer ben Horkenos, were in one scale of the balance, and Elazar ben Arach in the other, he would outweigh them all.

---

disciples that I have learned the most"   אמר ר' חנינא הרבה למדתי מרבותי ומחברי יותר מרבותי ומתלמידי יותר מכולם "Much have I learned from my teachers, still more from my colleagues, but most of all from my disciples" (Taanith 7a).

קנה לו שם טוב : Any other personal attainments, including ethical and spiritual values, will also benefit others to a great extent. But the profit inherent in a good name is of benefit chiefly, indeed almost exclusively, to him who has acquired it and will remain his on earth even after he himself has departed.

קנה לו דברי תורה implies that the individual has absorbed the words of the Torah to such a degree that they have become part and parcel of his thoughts and emotions and that he has learned how to apply them in study and in his personal development. According to the Sages, once the individual has reached this stage, the words of the Torah become "his own".

9–12.   In many cases the moral merit of one with less mental ability who has acquired only a modest amount of learning is greater by far than that of a superior intellect who has succeeded in gathering a great amount of knowledge. For the man of less mental ability can acquire his modest amount of knowledge only by dint of extraordinary effort and devotion. To the brilliant

יג אָמַר לָהֶם, צְאוּ וּרְאוּ אֵיזוֹ הִיא דֶרֶךְ טוֹבָה שֶׁיִּדְבַּק בָּהּ הָאָדָם,
רַבִּי אֱלִיעֶזֶר אוֹמֵר עַיִן טוֹבָה רַבִּי יְהוֹשֻׁעַ אוֹמֵר חָבֵר טוֹב רַבִּי
יוֹסֵי אוֹמֵר שָׁכֵן טוֹב רַבִּי שִׁמְעוֹן אוֹמֵר הָרוֹאֶה אֶת־הַנּוֹלָד רַבִּי
אֶלְעָזָר אוֹמֵר לֵב טוֹב: אָמַר לָהֶם רוֹאֶה אֲנִי אֶת־דִּבְרֵי אֶלְעָזָר
בֶּן־עֲרָךְ מִדִּבְרֵיכֶם שֶׁבִּכְלַל דְּבָרָיו דִּבְרֵיכֶם:

---

mind, on the other hand, learning comes very easily and his vast knowledge
is due primarily to his innate aptitude for learning. His sole merit is one which
he shares with the man of less ability whose store of knowledge is much
smaller than his; namely, that he has not wasted the talents with which his
Creator has endowed him but has used them in accordance with their purpose.
Coming from Yochanan ben Zakkai, who himself was a prototype of vast
erudition, who had many disciples and who, as a matter of fact, was the
bearer and preserver of the Torah after the collapse of the Jewish State, this
assertion is all the more significant. It was an admonition even to the most
proficient of his disciples to remain humble and to make the proper use of
their aptitudes, and at the same time a challenge to lesser talents to continue
their efforts undismayed. The five men described here in terms of their dom-
inant character traits were his most outstanding disciples. The posthumous
praise אשרי יולדתו which Yochanan ben Zakkai bestowed upon the mother of
Rabbi Yehoshua implies that Yehoshua was a man of moral and spiritual
excellence. It appears as if tradition was divided as to the relative merits
of Rabbi Eliezer ben Horkenos and Rabbi Elazar ben Arach, but this indecision
is only an apparent one. Actually, each has been accorded a position of equal
pre-eminence, equally justified, in his own field of knowledge. Rabbi Eliezer
ben Horkenos was superior in the faithful, loyal and accurate manner in
which he preserved the treasure of learning that had been handed down to
him. Rabbi Elazar ben Arach excelled in the ability to make broad application
of the Law and to draw from it a wealth of inferences for the shaping of
human affairs in accordance with the will of God as revealed to us. To be
sure, the qualities of ירא חטא and חסיד are demonstrated primarily in the
moral sphere, but they may be valid also in the area of scholarship. One who
is ירא חטא will be careful, above all, not to deliver himself of erroneous as-
sertions; conceit will not impel him to expound as a newly-discovered truth
an idea concerning which he himself still has secret doubts. When he realizes
the erroneous or even the doubtful character of a view he has propounded
he will not persist in it just because he once happened to set it forth. He will
never obstinately insist on his own views, but will be glad to be instructed by
others. One who is a perfect *chasid* will demonstrate his utter selflessness

13. He said to them: Go forth and see which is the good way to which a man should adhere. Rabbi Eliezer said: A good eye. Rabbi Yehoshua said: A good friend. Rabbi Yosé said: A good neighbor. Rabbi Shimon said: One who considers the consequences. Rabbi Elazar said: A good heart. He said to them: I prefer the words of Rabbi Elazar ben Arach to yours, because in his words yours are included.

---

also in the realm of scholarship. His sole concern will be the knowledge and the teaching of goodness and truth, regardless of whether the credit for its discovery will go to him or to some other man. Indeed, he will be glad to look into the view advanced by another, to test it, and to improve upon it; he will endeavor to find evidence and arguments in its support and will adopt it himself if it seems to him better than his own. We find innumerable instances of this character in the debates recorded in the Talmud.

13. Go forth into the realm of everyday life and search for a "way", a guiding principle to which a man should be able to adhere come what may in order to remain on the path that leads to the good. עין טובה, a "good eye" designates an attitude of kindness and good will toward all others, toward their concerns, their aspirations, their achievements and their possessions. A man with this attitude will rejoice when his fellow-man prospers; he will wish everyone well, and envy, jealousy, ill-will and rivalry will be utterly alien to him. "A good eye" should certainly keep us from placing obstacles into the path of the happiness and prosperity of our neighbor and should impel us gladly to do whatever may promote his welfare. It is self-evident that association with חבר טוב, a friend who desires only what is good, and—perhaps even more so because his proximity permits more frequent contact—with שכן טוב, a neighbor who desires only what is good, can provide us with a mighty bulwark against error and act as a potent help and support in our good endeavors. הרואה את הנולד : One who considers and foresees the consequences in whatever he may do will never become guilty of frivolous, irresponsible behavior. Fleeting attractions will not lead him astray, nor will immediate difficulties deter him from doing good. He will be able to foresee the bitter long-range consequences of sweet but fleeting pleasures; he will be mindful of the sense of bliss which can be purchased with every act of self-sacrificing devotion willingly performed, and therefore he will remain strong in the struggle against evil and mighty in doing good. The term לב טוב actually complies infinitely more than what is ordinarily thought of as a "good heart"; it involves much more that just kindness, readiness to perform good deeds and reluctance to turn down another's request. The term *lev* denotes a typically Jewish concept, the wellspring of *every* emotion, *every* aspiration, *every* endeavor, the source of *every* moral and spiritual impulse and tendency, **even** of all thought and character. Hence *lev* denotes the root and source of every

יד אָמַר לָהֶם, צְאוּ וּרְאוּ אֵיזוֹ הִיא דֶּרֶךְ רָעָה שֶׁיִּתְרַחֵק
מִמֶּנָּה הָאָדָם, רַבִּי אֱלִיעֶזֶר אוֹמֵר עַיִן רָעָה רַבִּי יְהוֹשֻׁעַ אוֹמֵר
חָבֵר רָע רַבִּי יוֹסֵי אוֹמֵר שָׁכֵן רָע רַבִּי שִׁמְעוֹן אוֹמֵר הַלֹּוֶה
וְאֵינוֹ מְשַׁלֵּם, אֶחָד הַלֹּוֶה מִן־הָאָדָם כְּלֹוֶה מִן־הַמָּקוֹם שֶׁנֶּאֱמַר
לֹוֶה רָשָׁע וְלֹא יְשַׁלֵּם וְצַדִּיק חוֹנֵן וְנוֹתֵן · רַבִּי אֶלְעָזָר אוֹמֵר
לֵב רָע: אָמַר לָהֶם, רוֹאֶה אֲנִי אֶת־דִּבְרֵי אֶלְעָזָר בֶּן־עֲרָךְ
מִדִּבְרֵיכֶם שֶׁבִּכְלַל דְּבָרָיו דִּבְרֵיכֶם:

טו הֵם אָמְרוּ שְׁלשָׁה דְבָרִים · רַבִּי אֱלִיעֶזֶר אוֹמֵר, יְהִי כְבוֹד
חֲבֵרְךָ חָבִיב עָלֶיךָ כְּשֶׁלָּךְ וְאַל־תְּהִי נוֹחַ לִכְעוֹס וְשׁוּב יוֹם אֶחָד
לִפְנֵי מִיתָתְךָ וֶהֱוֵה מִתְחַמֵּם כְּנֶגֶד אוּרָן שֶׁל־חֲכָמִים וֶהֱוֵה זָהִיר
בְּגַחַלְתָּן שֶׁלֹּא תִכָּוֶה שֶׁנְּשִׁיכָתָן נְשִׁיכַת שׁוּעָל וַעֲקִיצָתָן עֲקִיצַת
עַקְרָב וּלְחִישָׁתָן לְחִישַׁת שָׂרָף וְכָל־דִּבְרֵיהֶם כְּגַחֲלֵי אֵשׁ:

---

endeavor and every achievement. If, therefore, the "heart" is "good"; if the
"heart" is receptive only to the good and directed to the good alone, the *whole*
man will be under the rule of the good; he will not be *capable* of desiring
evil and will be ready for every good endeavor. Thus the characterization *lev*
tov truly defines all the paths and devices that lead toward the good.

14. עַיִן רָעָה, "an evil eye", denotes the opposite attitude. A man with "an evil
eye" will not only feel no joy but experience actual distress when others prosper, and will rejoice when others suffer loss and sorrow, grief and misery. A
person of this character, as well as לֵב רַע, שְׁכֵן רַע, חֲבֵר רַע represent so great a
danger to our own moral purity that we are not just forbidden to associate
with them but are told יִתְרַחֵק מִמֶּנָּה, to keep far away from them. We must
avoid any influence that may tarnish the character of our own "eye" and
heart and bring us closer to evil friends and evil neighbors. הַלֹּוֶה וְאֵינוֹ מְשַׁלֵּם.
This characterization implies the antithesis of the thoughtful attitude which
leads a man to weigh the consequences of whatever he is about to do. It
refers to the attitude of irresponsible thoughtlessness of him who never stops
to consider the heavy burden of debt which any neglect of duty places upon
our shoulders. Whatever we receive from this world—and indeed, the entire
Universe makes countless contributions to every breath we take on earth—is
only a loan granted us to help us strive for and bring about those goals by
means of which we advance the welfare of God's world in accordance with
His will as revealed to us in His Law. No one exists solely for himself, and

14. He said to them: Go and see which is the evil way from which a man should stand apart. Rabbi Eliezer said: An evil eye. Rabbi Yehoshua said: A bad friend. Rabbi Yosé said: A bad neighbor. Rabbi Shimon said: One who borrows and does not repay, regardless of whether he borrows from the Omnipresent or from men, for it is said, "A lawless man borrows and never repays his debt but a righteous man deals generously and is a giver." (Psalms 37:21). Rabbi Elazar said: An evil heart. Thereupon he said to them: I prefer the words of Rabbi Elazar ben Arakh to yours, because in his words yours are included.

15. They said three things: Rabbi Eliezer said: Let the honor of your friend be as dear to you as your own and be not easily moved to anger and repent one day before your death. Warm yourself by the fire of the sages but beware of their glowing coals lest you burn yourself, for the proscription in force as regards any injury done them is [like] the bite of the fox, the sting of the scorpion and the hiss of the serpent, and all their words are like coals of fire.

---

the greater the loan he has been granted, the greater his obligation and the sum total of achievement that may be expected of him in return. Therefore he who idles away his time in this world, who pays no regard to law or duty, who lives only for *himself* and for the satisfaction of his own needs, desires and caprices and is content to build his happiness at the expense of his fellow-men without ever thinking of the return which he is expected to make and for which God has created him, borrows from the world without repaying his debt. With every breath he takes he becomes more deeply indebted to the world, and the greater the wealth and pleasures he has borrowed, the greater and the more crushing will be the bankruptcy of his life which will be charged against him by God and by the world. There is hardly a better metaphor than לוה רשע ואינו משלם to denote thoughtlessness as opposed to צדיק חונן. רואה את הנולד ונותן. The righteous man is not so. Because he places his duty above all else and devotes his whole life to its fulfillment, striving solely to "do justice" to God and to His world, it is the world that owes him a debt of gratitude. And the fewer the goods and pleasures he has received from the world, the more does the world owe him, and it is usually as a major "creditor" that the *tzadik* departs from the earth.

15. Let the honor of your fellow man be as dear to you as your own. Therefore do not be quick to anger, lest your outburst of temper violate his honor. Rather than feeling anger at your friend's conduct, think of your own shortcomings and work unceasingly at the improvement of your own character. "Repent one day before your death;" regard every day as if it were your last, and mend your ways today because you have no way of knowing whether

טז רַבִּי יְהוֹשֻׁעַ אוֹמֵר, עַיִן הָרָע וְיֵצֶר הָרָע וְשִׂנְאַת הַבְּרִיּוֹת מוֹצִיאִין אֶת־הָאָדָם מִן־הָעוֹלָם:

יז רַבִּי יוֹסֵי אוֹמֵר, יְהִי מָמוֹן חֲבֵרְךָ חָבִיב עָלֶיךָ כְּשֶׁלָּךְ וְהַתְקֵן עַצְמְךָ לִלְמוֹד תּוֹרָה שֶׁאֵינָה יְרֻשָּׁה־לָךְ וְכָל־מַעֲשֶׂיךָ יִהְיוּ לְשֵׁם שָׁמָיִם:

---

you will still be alive tomorrow. You can hardly do more for the improvement of your character than make yourself familiar with teachings of the Sages and with the example they have set and follow their precepts. For their words give you not only light but warmth, supplying you with vigorous life and strength for every good endeavor. But beware of their "glowing coals!" Many a word they have uttered and many a precept they have ordained may seem to you outworn, extinct, "burned out", as it were, because the "fire" seems to have gone from it, and you may lay your hand irreverently upon it and toy with it at your pleasure. But it behooves you to look out, for not a word or precept of the Sages can ever become obsolete or lose its fiery force. That which seems burned out to you still holds within it an eternal flame and will burn the hand that would dare touch it with irreverence. The power of the pro-scription in force with regard to the words and precepts of the Sages is fre-quently portrayed in our sacred literature by the metaphor of the "bite" or "sting" that will afflict him who would dare wilfully to violate it. וכל דבריהם כגחלי אש they never turn into *gechalim* but remain *gachale esh* forever.

16. Any one of these three things is sufficient to cause a man to lose that position which he would be qualified to fill in the world: An evil eye which can never rejoice as long as it sees others prosper; an evil passion or vice which a man has permitted to gain ascendancy over him; and misanthropy which makes him scorn his fellowmen, making him aware only of the evil in others and causing him to overlook the good which is never entirely absent in any human being. The Sages use a beautiful expression to describe men in their admonitions to us to love mankind and to shun malice. They call our fellow-men בריות, "creatures" of God, and they employ this term to include all men, without exception, thus stressing the motive which is at the basis of the behest to love all men. We are to respect in a human being, whoever and whatever he may be, the "creature of God" and we must not deny this love to any fellowman, seeing that we were all made by the same Creator.

17. These three maxims are teachings that should guide us and keep us in the paths of goodness and truth in our relations with other human beings, in our attitude toward the Torah and, indeed, in every other aspect of our lives as well. Even as we take care to preserve our own wealth and to increase

16.   Rabbi Yehoshua said: An evil eye, evil passion and misanthropy put a man out of the world.

17.   Rabbi Yosé said: Let the property of your friend be as dear to you as your own; charge yourself to study the Torah, for it does not come to you by inheritance, and let everything you do be done to honor God.

---

it, so, too, it is not enough merely not to be envious of the wealth of our fellow-man or to view it with unconcern; we should be happy when he prospers, we must not stand by idly if we can guard him from injury and we should rejoice at any opportunity we may have to help him improve his lot.

We may have had the good fortune to have been born and reared by parents and in an environment that have not allowed us to remain strangers to the knowledge of the Torah and to the way of life that it demands. Indeed, the importance of the teaching and example set by the home in the acquisition of Torah in both theory and practice cannot be overestimated. However, we must always remember that the mere circumstance that the Torah has thus become our "inheritance" does not spell the completion of our own work in behalf of the Torah. In the case of wealth inherited from our parents we may indeed be satisfied with our inheritance as it stands, and while we will be careful to keep it intact, we are under no obligation to increase it by our own efforts. But in the case of Torah knowledge inherited by way of the training and guidance we have received from our parents, we must never be content to stand still. Rather, it is incumbent upon us, throughout our lives, to make continuous advances in the limitless realm of Torah wisdom, and the greater the fundamental inheritance of Torah knowledge that we have been privileged to take with us from the home of our parents into our own independent lives, the greater will be our obligation to continue building upon these foundations and by dint of our own efforts and the application of all our mental powers; to increase our portion in the everlasting spiritual treasure that the Torah is. It is self-understood, of course, that this admonition applies also, and indeed all the more so, to one who has not been so fortunate as to receive much Torah wisdom—or even any Torah knowledge at all—from the hands of his parents. התקן עצמך ללמוד תורה: discipline and train yourself, charge yourself to study the Torah. For the Torah is the spiritual treasure that belongs to the entire Jewish nation, a treasure in which every Jew is meant and required to assume an active share in accordance with his abilities. One who was not fortunate enough to receive training to this end in childhood is obligated to make up for this deficiency on his own accord in adolescence and adulthood, שאינה ירושה לך for the extent to which we fulfill our destiny for Torah must not be made merely dependent on the size of the Torah inheritance we have received from our parents. וכל מעשיך יהיו לשם שמים What-

יח רַבִּי שִׁמְעוֹן אוֹמֵר, הֱוֵי זָהִיר בִּקְרִיאַת שְׁמַע וּבִתְפִלָּה וּכְשֶׁאַתָּה מִתְפַּלֵּל אַל־תַּעַשׂ תְּפִלָּתְךָ קֶבַע אֶלָּא רַחֲמִים וְתַחֲנוּנִים לִפְנֵי הַמָּקוֹם שֶׁנֶּאֱמַר כִּי־חַנּוּן וְרַחוּם הוּא אֶרֶךְ אַפַּיִם וְרַב־חֶסֶד וְנִחָם עַל־הָרָעָה · וְאַל־תְּהִי רָשָׁע בִּפְנֵי עַצְמֶךָ :

יט רַבִּי אֶלְעָזָר אוֹמֵר, הֱוֵי שָׁקוּד לִלְמוֹד תּוֹרָה וְדַע מַה־שֶּׁתָּשִׁיב לְאֶפִּיקוֹרוֹס וְדַע לִפְנֵי מִי אַתָּה עָמֵל וּמִי הוּא בַּעַל מְלַאכְתְּךָ שֶׁיְּשַׁלֶּם־לָךְ שְׂכַר פְּעֻלָּתֶךָ :

כ רַבִּי טַרְפוֹן אוֹמֵר, הַיּוֹם קָצֵר וְהַמְּלָאכָה מְרֻבָּה וְהַפּוֹעֲלִים עֲצֵלִים וְהַשָּׂכָר הַרְבֵּה וּבַעַל הַבַּיִת דּוֹחֵק:

---

ever we do, we are to do *leshem shamayim*. Even the good that we do loses much of its value if we do not do it from a pure and God-oriented sense of duty, or if we are motivated in our action by expectations of personal advantage or honor. Indeed, the motive implied by the term *leshem shamayim* should dominate every aspect of our lives, even that phase which is devoted primarily to personal maintenance and to the care of our physical selves so that this side of our lives, too, may be lifted, as it should be, beyond the borders of the physical and the selfish into the realm of moral achievement and duty fulfilled in the service of God. In this manner all the phases of our lives will be preserved for the ways of goodness and purity that are in accord with our duty. As is stated in Prov. 3:6: בכל דרכיך דעהו והוא יישר ארחתיך "Have your mind directed to God in all your ways, and He will direct your path."

18. The שמע is addressed to you and therefore is clearly meant for you to take to your heart as you read it in prayerful reverence. In the same manner the words of prayer, though formally addressed directly to God, are designed to be taken to the heart of the worshipper so that their content may become part of his heart and mind and that the confessions, petitions and high resolutions expressed in them may become his own. It is only if he permits prayer thus to affect him that he can expect his prayer to be effective before God; he cannot expect that his prayer should perform that service for him if he performs it as קבע as an appointed routine act which was imposed upon him from some outside source and which can be properly discharged by rote recitation. ואל תהי רשע וכו' Do not allow yourself to be taken in by the erroneous idea advanced by alien philosophies that man on his own must of necessity be crushed by the weight of his guilt and that it is solely through the gracious

18. Rabbi Shimon said; Be careful in reading the *Shema* and in prayer, and when you pray, do not regard your prayer as an appointed routine but as an appeal for mercy and favor before the Omnipresent, as it is said: "For He is gracious and full of mercy, slow to anger and abundant in loving-kindness, and relenting of the evil decree"; and do not consider yourself as wicked when left to depend on your own efforts.

19. Rabbi Elazar said: Be diligent to study the Torah and know what to answer him who treats the Law with scorn. Know, too, before Whose countenance you are laboring and who your Employer is, who will pay you the reward for your labor.

20. Rabbi Tarphon said: The day is short, the task is great, the workmen are sluggish, the reward is great, and the Employer is insistent.

---

intercession of another that he can gain control over evil and be delivered from the burden of his sin. The one person able to free you from sin and to raise you to the level of pure and free devotion to duty in the service of God is none other than you yourself, and prayer uttered in the proper spirit will be that source from which you will derive the strength and Divine aid that you need in all your efforts at self-liberation from evil.

19. Only one who is not thoroughly familiar with the Torah will be afraid of the arguments advanced by אפיקורסים. One who has studied and continues to study the law adequately and thoroughly and delves into it with devotion will clearly see the speciousness and the invalidity of their allegations and will know that their arguments are founded on ignorance and distortion of facts. Know, too, under Whose supervision it is that you complete your life's task in study and practice alike and that He in Whose service you are laboring will not let your faithful toil go unrewarded.

20. Life is short and the task that each individual must complete on earth is great; yet men are slow to complete their work. They race in hot pursuit of pleasure as if they had only one day left to live but they are as slow in fulfilling their duty as if they had an eternity at their disposal for this purpose. Yet the reward we may expect is great and rich; it is a sense of God's approval and of His blessed nearness, the happy knowledge of duty loyally discharged, Divine aid in this life and bliss in the world to come. And if all this should not be sufficient incentive to conquer our laziness, then certainly the thought of the service we owe our Supreme Employer should spur us to vigorous action. For our Employer, Who is none other than God Himself, will not permit the work which He wants to see done to remain uncompleted because of our sluggishness. That which his workmen will refuse to do with

כא הוּא הָיָה אוֹמֵר, לֹא עָלֶיךָ הַמְּלָאכָה לִגְמוֹר וְלֹא־אַתָּה בֶן־
חוֹרִין לְהִבָּטֵל מִמֶּנָּה אִם לָמַדְתָּ תוֹרָה הַרְבֵּה נוֹתְנִין לְךָ שָׂכָר
הַרְבֵּה וְנֶאֱמָן הוּא בַּעַל מְלַאכְתְּךָ שֶׁיְשַׁלֶּם לְךָ שְׂכַר פְּעֻלָּתֶךָ וְדַע
שֶׁמַּתַּן שְׂכָרָן שֶׁל־צַדִּיקִים לֶעָתִיד לָבוֹא : רבי חנניא בן עקשיה וכו׳.

פרק שלישי
כל ישראל וכו׳.

א עֲקַבְיָא בֶּן־מַהֲלַלְאֵל אוֹמֵר הִסְתַּכֵּל בִּשְׁלֹשָׁה דְבָרִים וְאֵין
אַתָּה בָא לִידֵי עֲבֵרָה דַע מֵאַיִן בָּאתָ וּלְאָן אַתָּה הוֹלֵךְ וְלִפְנֵי מִי
אַתָּה עָתִיד לִתֵּן דִּין וְחֶשְׁבּוֹן · מֵאַיִן בָּאתָ מִטִּפָּה סְרוּחָה, וּלְאָן
אַתָּה הוֹלֵךְ לִמְקוֹם עָפָר רִמָּה וְתוֹלֵעָה, וְלִפְנֵי מִי אַתָּה עָתִיד
לִתֵּן דִּין וְחֶשְׁבּוֹן לִפְנֵי מֶלֶךְ מַלְכֵי הַמְּלָכִים הַקָּדוֹשׁ בָּרוּךְ הוּא ·

---

loyalty and dispatch, He will know how to force through despite their aversion for effort. The way of His world-wide rule is such that He is amply supplied with industrious servants and willing workers for His world order.

21. The good that God wants to see accomplished on earth is not all meant for one individual to complete. Any human being can contribute only one fraction to the whole, and it is only through the united efforts of all that the salvation to come into flower on earth can be brought about. But even though no one individual is capable of doing all the work by himself, each and every man is obligated to make his contribution to the full extent of his abilities. No one has a right to argue, "What I can do is but so little," and sit back idly. True, your contribution may not amount to much when measured against the task at hand, but as far as you are concerned it is very great; indeed, it represents the total content of your life. Even if you should remain alone in your good endeavors, continue to perform your round of duty faithfully and painstakingly, and leave it to your Employer to add your loyal and honest contribution to all the other resources which He employs to accomplish the work of salvation ordained through His will. If you accomplish a great deal, be it in study or in practice, you will receive your reward. Even if the greatest of your contributions is still not in excess of what was expected of you in accordance with the abilities and resources with which you have been endowed, and even if the utmost in devotion on your part yields only a fraction of the whole to be accomplished, your reward will be great nevertheless

21. He used to say: It is not up to you to complete the work, yet
you are not free to desist from it. If you have studied much Torah,
much reward will be given you, and your Employer is faithful to pay
you the reward for your work; but know that the reward of the
righteous will be in the world to come.

CHAPTER III

1. Akavyah ben Mahalalel said: Reflect upon three things, and you
will not come into the grip of sin: Know whence you came, where
you are going, and before Whom you will have to render account
and reckoning. *Whence you came*—from a putrid drop. *Where are
you going*—to a place of dust, of decay and vermin. *Before whom
you will have to render account and reckoning*—Before the Supreme
King of Kings, the Holy One, blessed be He.

---

in terms of the measure of your contribution. But do not seek to measure the
reward for good deeds by what man receives in this world. The true compensation is in store for him only in the world to come.

CHAPTER III

1. Most of our sins are outgrowths of an over-emphasis of the sensuous
physical aspects of our being and of their demands, and of a disregard. or at
least, of insufficient regard for the spiritual and moral facets of our personality
and its purpose. We must bear in mind at all times that, someday, we will
be called upon to render strict accounting for the manner in which we fulfilled,
or failed to fulfill, this our purpose. We are reminded, too, that our whole
sensuous bodily being is doomed to decay from the very beginning. It is only
the spiritual and moral element within us, that part of us which is conscious
of its destiny and is capable of decision and judgment over our actions, that
will survive the decay of the purely physical and will enter into eternity.
There it will render accounting as to the extent to which it has achieved its
destiny on earth, and as to the manner in which it has husbanded the resources
and the faculties with which it had been endowed for this purpose. And the
One before Whom this accounting is to be made is none other than He Who
is the absolute Ruler over all things and Who is fully able· to ensure for
Himself the ultimate total obedience of all things and all men.

ב רַבִּי חֲנִינָא סְגַן הַכֹּהֲנִים אוֹמֵר, הֱוֵי מִתְפַּלֵּל בִּשְׁלוֹמָהּ שֶׁל־מַלְכוּת שֶׁאַלְמָלֵא מוֹרָאָהּ אִישׁ אֶת־רֵעֵהוּ חַיִּים בְּלָעוֹ:

ג רַבִּי חֲנַנְיָא בֶּן־תְּרַדְיוֹן אוֹמֵר, שְׁנַיִם שֶׁיּוֹשְׁבִין וְאֵין בֵּינֵיהֶם דִּבְרֵי תוֹרָה הֲרֵי זֶה מוֹשַׁב לֵצִים שֶׁנֶּאֱמַר וּבְמוֹשַׁב לֵצִים לֹא יָשָׁב. אֲבָל שְׁנַיִם שֶׁיּוֹשְׁבִין וְיֵשׁ בֵּינֵיהֶם דִּבְרֵי תוֹרָה שְׁכִינָה שְׁרוּיָה בֵּינֵיהֶם שֶׁנֶּאֱמַר אָז נִדְבְּרוּ יִרְאֵי יְיָ אִישׁ אֶל־רֵעֵהוּ וַיַּקְשֵׁב יְיָ וַיִּשְׁמָע וַיִּכָּתֵב סֵפֶר זִכָּרוֹן לְפָנָיו לְיִרְאֵי יְיָ וּלְחֹשְׁבֵי שְׁמוֹ. אֵין לִי אֶלָּא שְׁנַיִם, מִנַּיִן אֲפִלּוּ אֶחָד שֶׁיּוֹשֵׁב וְעוֹסֵק בַּתּוֹרָה שֶׁהַקָּדוֹשׁ בָּרוּךְ הוּא קוֹבֵעַ לוֹ שָׂכָר שֶׁנֶּאֱמַר יֵשֵׁב בָּדָד וְיִדֹּם כִּי נָטַל עָלָיו:

2. Actually, the three considerations given in the Mishna immediately preceding should be sufficient deterrents from all sin and excesses, even without the intervention of a human authority and, in fact, they are sufficient for him who has remained pure. But human society is still in that state of moral imperfection where it fears even the lowliest visible human authority more than the unseen omnipotence of the King of Kings. Hence the orderly, undisturbed development towards that happiness to which all men are entitled is dependent upon the preservation of the authority of earthly powers and officials. Therefore, respect the authorities of the place and of the country in which you reside, and pray for their welfare. This duty was enjoined upon the Jew when he first left his homeland to dwell in the midst of the many nations of the world (see Jeremiah 29:7). We are obliged not only לדרוש, to do everything to promote the welfare of the countries in which we live, but actually להתפלל, to pray, before God and as good citizens, with sincere devotion known and recognized as such by Him alone, to beseech Him for the welfare of the government. For if the government could not exercise its authority, the hand of everyone would be lifted up against all the others and all of society would disintegrate

3. לצים are the foes of God's Law who, by glibness of speech, undermine the respect and reverence in which the Torah should be held. Now it is evident from the words אז נדברו which is quoted and ליראי ה' ולחשבי שמו in the sentence explained here, that the term *divrei Torah* should be construed in a broader sense than just the "words" of Torah, the study and explanation of God's Law. For the verse speaks not of למודי ה', but of יראי ה' and חושבי שמו, and

2. Rabbi Chaninah, the Assistant of the High-Priests, said: Pray for the welfare of the government, for were it not for the fear of it, men would swallow each other alive.

3. Rabbi Chananyah, ben Teradyon, said: If two sit together and words of Torah are not exchanged between them, this is a "seat of the scornful", as it is said, "And he never sat there where the scornful sit." But if two sit together and interchange words of Torah, the Presence of God abides with them, for it is said, "They that feared *God* spoke with one another, and *God* noted and heard, and a book of remembrance was written before Him for those who fear *God* and think upon His Name." This verse refers to two people. How, then, can we know that even if one person sits and occupies himself with the Torah, the Holy One, blessed be He, will determine a reward for him? Because it is said: "Though he may sit alone, let his mind be at rest, for he has received that which was appointed for him."

---

these are designations denoting practical fulfillment rather than mere theoretical study. According to the Sages, too (see Berachoth 6a), the חושבי שמו are those whose intentions are upon the fulfillment of a mitzvah. On this they base the teaching that חשב אדם לעשות מצוה ונאנס ולא עשאה מעלה עליו הכתוב כאילו עשאה, if a person had in mind to perform a mitzvah, then, even if he would be prevented from carrying out his good intention, it would be counted as if he had actually succeeded in fulfilling his high resolve. Or, as we read in Kiddushin 40a, מחשבה טובה מצרפה למעשה, any good thought that, through unavoidable circumstances, could not be translated into action, is nevertheless counted by God as part of the good deed. Besides, the term *divrei Torah* cannot properly be interpreted here in its narrow sense. The place where people deliberate on how best to perform a mitzvah is certainly not a *moshav letzim*. As a matter of fact, Yaavetz notes in connection with this Mishna that even a discussion of anything necessary for human life cannot possibly be classed as a *moshav letzim*. Rather, our Mishna refers to people who, instead of occupying themselves with *divrei Torah,* talk דברים בטלים, of such things as are of absolutely no use and no value. We believe, that the meaning of *divrei Torah* would include not only the actual teaching contained in the Torah itself, but also everything else that derives from the Torah for the fashioning of human affairs, as well as anything that is shaped in accordance with the Torah's teachings and is fulfilled in accordance with the spirit of the Law of God. But those who, instead of turning their thoughts to the serious things of life, in the broadest sense, waste their leisure time on frivolity and worthless trifles, their assembly is indeed classed by the Mishna as *moshav letzim* even

ד רַבִּי שִׁמְעוֹן אוֹמֵר, שְׁלֹשָׁה שֶׁאָכְלוּ עַל שֻׁלְחָן אֶחָד וְלֹא אָמְרוּ עָלָיו דִּבְרֵי תוֹרָה כְּאִלּוּ אָכְלוּ מִזִּבְחֵי מֵתִים שֶׁנֶּאֱמַר כִּי כָל־שֻׁלְחָנוֹת מָלְאוּ קִיא צוֹאָה בְּלִי מָקוֹם · אֲבָל שְׁלֹשָׁה שֶׁאָכְלוּ עַל שֻׁלְחָן אֶחָד וְאָמְרוּ עָלָיו דִּבְרֵי תוֹרָה כְּאִלּוּ אָכְלוּ מִשֻּׁלְחָנוֹ שֶׁל־מָקוֹם · שֶׁנֶּאֱמַר וַיְדַבֵּר אֵלַי זֶה הַשֻּׁלְחָן אֲשֶׁר לִפְנֵי יְיָ:

ה רַבִּי חֲנִינָא בֶּן־חֲכִינַאי אוֹמֵר, הַנֵּעוֹר בַּלַּיְלָה וְהַמְהַלֵּךְ בַּדֶּרֶךְ יְחִידִי וּמְפַנֶּה לִבּוֹ לְבַטָּלָה הֲרֵי זֶה מִתְחַיֵּב בְּנַפְשׁוֹ:

---

if, in fact, their words are not, strictly taken, in contempt of the Torah. For the failure as such to discuss *divrei Torah* is in itself an indication of disregard for the Torah, since it is said: במושב לצים לא ישב כי אם בתורת ה' חפצו וגו', "He never sat in the seat of the letzim, because, instead, he strove after the teaching of the Lord, and all his thoughts moved within His teachings both day and night." We read in Sanhedrin 99a that כל שאפשר לו לעסוק בתורה ואינו עוסק, "He who could occupy himself with the Torah but does not do so is counted among those of whom it is said: כי דבר ה' בזה."

4. Sanhedrin 3a presumes the knowledge of the Law among our people to be so widespread that any three adult Jewish males are deemed capable and qualified to act as a judicial tribunal to decide on matters of property, for אי אפשר דלית בהו חד דגמיר it is taken for granted that surely at least one of these three must have adequate knowledge of what is right and wrong according to the Law. Therefore, if three eat together at a table, it is presumed that at least one of them will not be entirely ignorant of the Teaching of God. If nevertheless, their meal will not be enhanced with even one word of Torah, of things of the spirit, then that meal was not worthy of a human being. In such a case, the meal, instead of being a part of the spiritual and moral aspects of living, is only an act of animal gratification in which the purely human element is not seen. זבחי מתים are sacrificial meals that were offered to the idols representing that lack of freedom which the heathens worshipped. It is the term employed in the Psalms (Psalm 106:28) to denote the ceremonial meals dedicated to *Peor*, the god of degenerate shamelessness. זה השולחן אשר לפני ה' (Ezechiel 41:22) refers to the *mizbe'ach* which had been named and described previously. From this, Berachoth 55a derives the teaching that "As long as the Temple still stood, the altar wrought atonement for Israel." Indeed, we may rightly say that the prime feature distinguishing man from the beast and rendering him civilized is the table at which men eat together. When the

4. Rabbi Shimon said: If three ate at a table and did not utter one word of Torah there, it is as if they had partaken of meal offerings made to the dead, for it is said, "All the tables are filled with execrable things without room [for aught else]." But if three have eaten at a table and uttered words of Torah there, it is as if they had eaten at the table of God, for it is said, "He said to me: This is the table which is before the countenance of *God*."

5. Rabbi Chanina ben Chachinai, said: He who keeps awake at night, and he who goes on his way alone, and makes room in his heart for idleness, sins against his own soul.

---

animal eats, it thinks only of itself and views any other animal that eats with it as a rival. Man is not so; he will not even enjoy his meal if he must eat it alone. He feels a real need to eat together with others. And the act of sharing a meal with his fellow-man reminds him at once that even the physical aspects of his body were not created for his own pleasure. This warning takes on even greater meaning and solemnity by virtue of the ברכת הזמון, the joint grace after meals to which our sages have attached so much significance. If then, as is presumed in this passage of Tractate Berachoth, this sense of brotherhood finds expression in the fact that the master of the house prepares the table not only for himself and the members of his household but also for the poor and needy, and if, as our Mishna likewise presupposes, the physical enjoyment of food is accompanied by spiritual nourishment from the Word of God, that table is truly one consecrated to the cultivation of human virtues and Divine teachings of which it can be rightly said זה השולחן אשר לפני ה'. Those who dined at this table have, in fact, eaten from God's own board, as it were, since they have partaken not only of the physical food but also of the moral and spiritual nourishment which God has apportioned for man who serves Him. In like manner it is written concerning the priests who received for their sustenance the portions of the sacrifices consecrated by the altar: משולחן גבוה קזכו.

5. A man who keeps awake at night because he cannot sleep, or one who walks on his way alone, has perfect, undisturbed leisure during those lone and wakeful hours. He who, instead of utilizing those quiet moments for serious meditation and reflection, wastes them on frivolous and idle thoughts, sins against his own soul. For in this manner he has cheated his soul of spiritual and moral gains which it would have had the opportunity thus to acquire, and, at the same time, he has exposed it to all the perils which idle thoughts so easily engender.

י רַבִּי נְחוּנְיָא בֶּן־הַקָּנָה אוֹמֵר, כָּל־הַמְקַבֵּל עָלָיו עוֹל תּוֹרָה
מַעֲבִירִין מִמֶּנּוּ עוֹל מַלְכוּת וְעוֹל דֶּרֶךְ אֶרֶץ וְכָל־הַפּוֹרֵק מִמֶּנּוּ
עוֹל תּוֹרָה נוֹתְנִין עָלָיו עוֹל מַלְכוּת וְעוֹל דֶּרֶךְ אֶרֶץ:

ז רַבִּי חֲלַפְתָּא בֶּן־דּוֹסָא אִישׁ כְּפַר חֲנַנְיָא אוֹמֵר, עֲשָׂרָה
שֶׁיּוֹשְׁבִין וְעוֹסְקִין בַּתּוֹרָה שְׁכִינָה שְׁרוּיָה בֵּינֵיהֶם שֶׁנֶּאֱמַר
אֱלֹהִים נִצָּב בַּעֲדַת־אֵל· וּמִנַּיִן אֲפִלּוּ חֲמִשָּׁה שֶׁנֶּאֱמַר וַאֲגֻדָּתוֹ
עַל־אֶרֶץ יְסָדָהּ· וּמִנַּיִן אֲפִלּוּ שְׁלֹשָׁה שֶׁנֶּאֱמַר בְּקֶרֶב אֱלֹהִים
יִשְׁפֹּט· וּמִנַּיִן אֲפִלּוּ שְׁנַיִם שֶׁנֶּאֱמַר אָז נִדְבְּרוּ יִרְאֵי יְיָ אִישׁ אֶל־
רֵעֵהוּ וַיַּקְשֵׁב יְיָ וַיִּשְׁמָע· וּמִנַּיִן אֲפִלּוּ אֶחָד שֶׁנֶּאֱמַר בְּכָל־הַמָּקוֹם
אֲשֶׁר אַזְכִּיר אֶת־שְׁמִי אָבֹא אֵלֶיךָ וּבֵרַכְתִּיךָ:

ח רַבִּי אֶלְעָזָר אִישׁ בַּרְתּוֹתָא אוֹמֵר, תֶּן־לוֹ מִשֶּׁלּוֹ שֶׁאַתָּה

---

6. The Jew has a dual burden to bear. First, there is that additional burden, which the government of the country in which he resides imposes upon him because it treats him as a stranger within its territory. Secondly, along with all others, he bears the burden which day-to-day secular living entails. He who freely submits to the yoke of the Torah, who will put all of his thoughts and actions in the service of the Torah, will not feel oppressed by these burdens. In fact, he will accept and bear them cheerfully as part of the purpose ordained for him by God Himself. He who shrugs off the Torah service which he owes his God, even as he would cast off a yoke imposed upon him, may indeed imagine that he has freed himself. However, he fails to see that it is precisely under these circumstances that all the other cares of his life as a citizen and as a member of society will weigh upon him as crushing burdens. For once he has cast off the yoke of the Law, he will lack the staying power which can be derived only from serving the Torah; he will lack that serene contentment and vitality which can be gained only through service of the Torah.

7. Any group of ten men united in accordance with the spirit of· Judaism for truly Jewish causes constitutes a "congregation" and represents, on a small scale, the entire Jewish community. When such men occupy themselves jointly with the study of the Torah and the endeavor to understand the tasks it has set them, they are an עדת אל, a "congregation of the Almighty." God is present in their midst, for, according to the verse from the Psalms quoted here, God נצב "stands ready" to intervene in behalf of "His own" congrega-

6. Rabbi Nechunyah ben Hakanah, said: He who takes upon himself the yoke of the Torah, from him the yoke of the government and the yoke of secular life will be removed. But he who casts off the yoke of the Torah, upon him will be laid the yoke of the government and the yoke of secular life.

7. Rabbi Chalaftah ben Dosa, of the village of Chananyah, said: When ten people sit together and occupy themselves with the Torah, the Presence of God dwells among them, for it is said, "God stands in a congregation of the Almighty." And whence can it be shown that the same applies also to five? Because it is said: "He has founded His band upon earth." And whence can it be shown that the same applies even to three? Because it is said: "He judges in the midst of judges." And whence can it be shown that it applies even to two? Because it is said, "Then those who feared *God* spoke one with the other and *God* listened and heard." And whence can it be shown that it applies even to one? Because it is said: "In any place where I shall cause My Name to be remembered, I will come to you and bless you."

8. Rabbi Elazar of Barthotha said: Give Him what is His, because

---

tion, protecting and reigning, furthering and aiding, even as it is written of *Yaakov*, who lives on in every *kehilath Yaakov* to this very day: והנה ה' נצב עליו. Even five people who have banded together in this spirit for these purposes represent אגדתו, a "godly band". It is God, His word and His will, that has united them , and על ארץ יסדה it is He that gives their union a firm foundation and endurance, support and soundness on earth. And even if it is only three that have joined in the effort to glean from the Torah the standard of truth and right for the orderly development of human affairs and to enforce that standard by righteous sentence, God will abide with them and guide their study and their understanding so that their pronouncements will be in accordance with His own word. In fact, even when there are only two God-fearing men who occupy themselves with the word of God and who discuss its contents and the tasks that it poses, God will listen and will not allow even one of their words that genuinely seeks after truth to pass in vain. Indeed even the one person who sits alone and occupies himself with the Torah, is told: "In every place where I, God, cause My Name to be mentioned, wherever you are impelled to declare My Name not out of delusion, caprice or folly, but for My own sake, for the sake of My word, My teaching and the fulfillment of My command, I will come to you and bless you. I shall bless your study, your endeavors and your achievements."

8. All that you are and all that you have belongs to God, for whatever you

וְשֶׁלְּךָ שֶׁלּוֹ וְהֵן בְּיָדוֹ הוּא אוֹמֵר כִּי־מִמְּךָ הַכֹּל וּמִיָּדְךָ נָתַנּוּ לָךְ:

י רַבִּי יַעֲקֹב אוֹמֵר, הַמְהַלֵּךְ בַּדֶּרֶךְ וְשׁוֹנֶה וּמַפְסִיק מִמִּשְׁנָתוֹ וְאוֹמֵר מַה־נָּאֶה אִילָן זֶה מַה־נָּאֶה נִיר זֶה מַעֲלֶה עָלָיו הַכָּתוּב כְּאִלּוּ מִתְחַיֵּב בְּנַפְשׁוֹ:

י רַבִּי דוֹסְתַּאי בַּר יַנַּאי מִשּׁוּם רַבִּי מֵאִיר אוֹמֵר, כָּל־הַשּׁוֹכֵחַ דָּבָר אֶחָד מִמִּשְׁנָתוֹ מַעֲלֶה עָלָיו הַכָּתוּב כְּאִלּוּ מִתְחַיֵּב בְּנַפְשׁוֹ שֶׁנֶּאֱמַר רַק הִשָּׁמֶר לְךָ וּשְׁמֹר נַפְשְׁךָ מְאֹד פֶּן־תִּשְׁכַּח אֶת־הַדְּבָרִים אֲשֶׁר־רָאוּ עֵינֶיךָ · יָכוֹל אֲפִילוּ תָּקְפָה עָלָיו מִשְׁנָתוֹ תַּלְמוּד לוֹמַר וּפֶן־יָסוּרוּ מִלְּבָבְךָ כֹּל יְמֵי חַיֶּיךָ, הָא אֵינוֹ מִתְחַיֵּב בְּנַפְשׁוֹ עַד־שֶׁיֵּשֵׁב וִיסִירֵם מִלִּבּוֹ:

יא רַבִּי חֲנִינָא בֶּן־דּוֹסָא אוֹמֵר, כָּל שֶׁיִּרְאַת חֶטְאוֹ קוֹדֶמֶת לְחָכְמָתוֹ חָכְמָתוֹ מִתְקַיֶּמֶת וְכָל שֶׁחָכְמָתוֹ קוֹדֶמֶת לְיִרְאַת חֶטְאוֹ אֵין חָכְמָתוֹ מִתְקַיֶּמֶת:

may be and whatever you may possess you have received from Him alone. If you will keep this thought before you at all times, then you will be ready, gladly and at any time, to muster all your physical and spiritual faculties and resources in the service of the fulfillment of His will. Then you will never find it within your heart to pride yourself on what you have given or on what you have achieved, for you will know that you could have neither given nor achieved without having received the strength and the means from Him, and that whatever has been given you, you have received only for the purpose of employing it to do the will of God.

9. ‏מִשְׁנָתוֹ,‏ "his" teaching, that teaching which deals with man's voluntary shaping of his own life and of his own affairs in accordane with the will of his Creator and Master, a teaching which lends to human life and development a harmony, perfection and moral splendor before which the physical beauties of nature all recede into the shadows. For what does this teaching do but build the most intimate unity out of the most diverse variety of human life experiences through the free permeation of the latter with the Divine spirit in accordance with the will of God, a harmony which realizes the concept of beauty in the most sublime sense of the word. This Mishna teaches us the

you and all that you have are His. Thus it is said by David: "All things come from You and of Your own we have given You."

9. Rabbi Yaakov said: He who is walking by the way and studies and breaks off his study and exclaims: "How beautiful is this tree!" "How fine is that field!" is regarded as if he had sinned against his own soul.

10. Rabbi Dostai bar Yannai, said, in the name of Rabbi Meir: Whosoever forgets [even] one word of his study, him the Scripture regards as if he had sinned against his soul; for it is said: "Only take heed of yourself and guard your soul diligently that you may not forget the facts which your eyes have beheld." Now one might suppose that the same result would follow even if the retention of what he has studied has been too hard for him. To guard against such an inference, the Torah adds "And lest they depart from your heart all the days of your life." Accordingly, he is guilty of sinning against his soul only if he sits down idly and deliberately removes [these teachings] from his heart.

11. Rabbi Chanina ben Dosa, said: He in whom the fear of sin goes before his wisdom, his wisdom shall endure; but he in whom wisdom precedes the fear of sin, his wisdom will not endure.

---

following great lesson: He who, while studying, does not become aware of this higher beauty of God's teaching, so that he will break off his sacred work to exclaim over the beauty of nature, is as if he had sinned against his own soul, or, rather, as if he had forfeited his soul. For, despite his study, he thus shows that he has not come to understand the dignity and beauty of a human soul that is guided and enlightened by the spirit of God; a beauty and dignity that surpasses all earthly beauty by far.

10. That which is said primarily concerning the historical fact of the Revelation of the Law, an event which we ourselves have experienced, and which we are bidden to keep before us always and never to allow to depart from our minds, is applied here also to the actual contents of that revealed Law. With solemn rigor we are held responsible for every word of the contents of the Law which we might indeed have studied but then forgotten due to negligence, indolence or indifference.

11. The "fear of sin", the fear of committing some act that would not be in accordance with the will of God, is a direct outgrowth and practical demonstration of the "fear of God". The fear of God and the fear of sin are character qualities which are not dependent upon wisdom and erudition, but which, in fact, must come before these intellectual gifts if the wisdom and erudition

יג הוּא הָיָה אוֹמֵר, כֹּל שֶׁמַּעֲשָׂיו מְרֻבִּים מֵחָכְמָתוֹ חָכְמָתוֹ מִתְקַיֶּמֶת וְכֹל שֶׁחָכְמָתוֹ מְרֻבָּה מִמַּעֲשָׂיו אֵין חָכְמָתוֹ מִתְקַיֶּמֶת:

יג הוּא הָיָה אוֹמֵר, כֹּל שֶׁרוּחַ הַבְּרִיּוֹת נוֹחָה הֵימֶנּוּ רוּחַ הַמָּקוֹם נוֹחָה הֵימֶנּוּ וְכֹל שֶׁאֵין רוּחַ הַבְּרִיּוֹת נוֹחָה הֵימֶנּוּ אֵין רוּחַ הַמָּקוֹם נוֹחָה הֵימֶנּוּ:

יד רַבִּי דוֹסָא בֶּן־הָרְכִּינַס אוֹמֵר, שֵׁנָה שֶׁל־שַׁחֲרִית וְיַיִן שֶׁל־צָהֳרַיִם וְשִׂיחַת הַיְלָדִים וִישִׁיבַת בָּתֵּי כְנֵסִיּוֹת שֶׁל־עַמֵּי הָאָרֶץ מוֹצִיאִין אֶת־הָאָדָם מִן־הָעוֹלָם:

are to be true and of the right kind. Particularly the wisdom of the Torah to which the term חכמה primarily refers here, can be properly grasped only by him who regards it as the God-given source of truth and duty. It can be truly understood only by him who approaches its study with the desire and the high resolve to derive from it guidance for understanding and a standard for his conduct, and protection against error and sin in theory or practice. As such a person walks on the road of life, his wisdom will gain in clarity with every step he takes; it will grow in the power to guide and to discipline, and to afford his soul blissful satisfaction, and it will walk beside him as his most faithful companion until the very end of his days. But he whose approach to wisdom and knowledge is devoid of the fear of God and the fear of sin, to whom the fear of God and the fear of sin are only to proceed from his wisdom, he will neither gain true wisdom nor acquire the genuine fear of God. He will regard every word of the Torah's wisdom only as a hindrance and impediment to the imagined freedom that he has enjoyed heretofore. He will distort its contents for his own purposes, changing and perverting them to suit his own view of life which is estranged from God—to what extent is immaterial—and finally he will discard it altogether as useless ballast and ignore it as an inconvenient intruder upon his freedom.

12. This verse is a continuation and a supplement of what has gone before. Here we are told: There are also persons who, though having adopted the right approach to the study of the Torah, nevertheless shall never attain true and enduring wisdom. Such a person may indeed have sought help in enriching and improving his understanding, and guidance for his life's duty from the Torah, but, if in practical life he lacks the strength to translate the knowledge of what is right into proper conduct, his wisdom cannot endure. Such a man may know what his duty is, but if he does not perform it in practice, or at

12.   He used to say: He whose deeds exceed his wisdom, his wisdom shall endure, but he whose wisdom exceeds his deeds, his wisdom will not endure.

13.   He used to say: He who is pleasing to his fellow-men is pleasing also to God; and he who is not pleasing to men is also displeasing to God.

14.   Rabbi Dosa ben Harkinas, said: Morning sleep and midday wine, children's talk and sitting in the assembly houses of the ignorant put a man out of the world.

---

least not to the extent to which he knows he should be doing it, and thus is rich in wisdom but poor in deeds, his wisdom has no permanence. It is stunted because it does not reach that stage of bloom and fruition in which it must be proven and in which alone it can attain its true worth and value. Accordingly, the sages have also said elsewhere: לימוד גדול שהלימוד מביא לידי מעשה "Study is great, for study leads to deeds," and לא המדרש עיקר אלא המעשה "The main thing is not inquiry, but deeds."

13.   The designation of מקום for God implies the universal relationship of God to the world. God is מקומו של עולם; He supports the world; it is through Him that the world endures. The designation for "man", which embraces all of mankind, regardless of individual differences, is בריות, literally, "creations". God created men for a   universal union. Even as all men, being the creatures of God, enjoy the same relationship to Him Who is their sole Creator and are united through Him, so despite all the many ways in which individuals differ from one another, men should draw closer to one another and each one should accept all the good found in the others so that, eventually, they will all form one single union of human beings beneath the reign of the Father of all Mankind. Therefore it is not in keeping with God's will that any one person should separate himself from all the others. True we may differ from one another with regard to principles and inalienable convictions which each of us must steadfastly keep and follow for himself, and as a consequence, also with regard to the way of life we must adopt. Yet there is possible a way of living together that all of us can accept, so that no one may become unpleasant and burdensome, hostile or unkind to the other, but that, instead, each of us may find pleasure in the company of the other and feel drawn to him. Unkind and hostile conduct toward other men is displeasing also to God and is in direct contradiction to the goals intended by God to be attained through mankind's life together. If you are really wiser, better and nobler than the others, then strive also to be more pleasant and amiable, so that people will like to be near you and absorb into their own personalities some of your wisdom, goodness and moral nobility.

14.   It is obvious that he who sleeps away the morning hours, who at noon

טו רַבִּי אֶלְעָזָר הַמּוֹדָעִי אוֹמֵר, הַמְחַלֵּל אֶת־הַקֳּדָשִׁים וְהַמְבַזֶּה
אֶת־הַמּוֹעֲדוֹת וְהַמַּלְבִּין פְּנֵי חֲבֵרוֹ בָּרַבִּים וְהַמֵּפֵר בְּרִיתוֹ שֶׁל־
אַבְרָהָם אָבִינוּ וְהַמְגַלֶּה פָנִים בַּתּוֹרָה שֶׁלֹּא כַהֲלָכָה, אַף עַל פִּי
שֶׁיֵּשׁ בְּיָדוֹ תּוֹרָה וּמַעֲשִׂים טוֹבִים, אֵין לוֹ חֵלֶק לָעוֹלָם הַבָּא:

---

dulls his mental clarity and alertness by indulging in strong drink, and who
wastes his evenings with childish trifles or at the tavern, will not have much
time left to devote to the earnest endeavor to fulfill the purpose for which
he has been put into the world. It is not unlikely that the Mishna frowns upon
each of these four idle pursuits separately as a thoughtless squandering of
time—that most precious gift that has been given man; time granted him for
the dutiful and faithful completion of life's task.

15. In Sanhedrin 99a this Mishna is quoted as follows: המחלל את הקדשים והמבזה
את המועדות והמפר בריתו של אברהם אבינו והמגלה פנים בתורה וכו' והמלבין פני חברו ברבים
The holy objects in the Temple, the Festivals and the rite of circumcision are
Divinely-established institutions through which the awareness of the holy
purpose of the individual and the community, and convictions and resolves for
its loyal and dutiful realization, are to be held fast, maintained and protected
from any misinterpretation and distortion not only for the present but for all
the generations to come. They are named here in the reverse chronological
order of their creation. All mo'adim, which are based on yetziat Mitzrayim,
preceded the erection of the mishkan. בריתו של אברהם אבינו marked the beginning
of our very existence as a nation. The bedrock and source of this knowledge
is the Torah. Before the election of Abraham, the awareness of man's moral
destiny was derived from man's consciousness of his general dignity as the
creature made in the image of God. Now this Mishna deems it possible that
one might think that a person might attain a certain degree of Torah wisdom
and also perform good deeds even though he disregards קדשים, מועדות and
מילה, and actually has a negative attitude to these sacred institutions, and has
no understanding at all of the inalienable higher Godly dignity of man. Yet
the Mishna tells us that notwithstanding his knowledge and good deeds a
person such as this has forfeited his portion in the world to come. For the
great basic Jewish institutions, the holy objects in the Temple, the Festivals,
the rite of circumcision, the revealed Word of God and the teaching that man
was made in God's image were all given to each one of us not simply as a
means for our own personal moral and spiritual advancement. They are much
more important than that; they represent the great Divine treasure entrusted
to us for the spiritual and moral improvement of our Jewish community and of

15.   Rabbi Elazar Ha-Mudai, said: He who profanes sacred things, who neglects the festivals, who humiliates his fellow-man in public and violates the covenant of Avraham, our father, and who interprets the Torah in a manner contradictory to the Halachah—though he may have the knowledge of Torah and good deeds—has no share in the world to come.

---

the larger community of mankind. We, as messengers, instruments and priests of the Kingdom of God that is to come upon earth, are to defend this treasure with our heart's blood and we are to put all of our thoughts, our ambitions and achievements into the endeavor to promote the ever-increasing recognition and acknowledgment of it. Therefore he who neglects any one of these Divinely-appointed institutions is guilty of contributing to the undermining of the future of God's kingdom on earth. Hence, regardless of any spiritual or moral qualities he might possess, he has forfeited his share in the eternity of the world to come.

In Sanhedrin 99a all these five transgressions are included in the pronouncement כי דבר ה' בזה; they are viewed as a show of disdain for the word of God. For, since they serve the perpetuation and realization of the Word of God on earth, the five sacred institutions to which reference is made and against which these sins have been committed, are emanations of the Word of God. מלבין פני חברו ברבים is the gravest of all sins against the dignity and nobleness inherent in every human being by virtue of the fact that he was made in the image of God. According to Sanhedrin 99b the term מגלה. פנים בתורה may also have an interpretation other than that offered here. According to that source, *panim* would not indicate the *interpretation* of the Torah as it does in many instances; e.g. in the sentence מ"ט פנים לתורה. Instead, *panim* would be construed in its literal meaning of "countenance", and thus the term גלוי פנים would indicate the opposite of הסתרת פנים (hiding one's face, an expression of modesty)—in other words, it would denote "impudence" or "impertinence". (Targum to Exod. 14:8 and Num. 15:30 renders ביד רמה by the term בריש גלי which means "with head uncovered"). Thusly interpreted, מגלה פנים בתורה would mean to treat the Torah with impudence and impertinence. One example of such behavior would be מבזה תלמידי חכמים the insulting and slighting of teachers of the Torah. This would include even מבזה חברו בפני תלמיד חכם, an instance where a person has so little respect for a תלמיד חכם, that, he would deliberately humiliate a fellow-man even in the presence of such a sage. If we accept this interpretation, the explanation of שלא כהלכה would present some difficulty. Apparently, the Talmud, according to this interpretation, generally omits these two words.

טז רַבִּי יִשְׁמָעֵאל אוֹמֵר, הֱוֵי קַל לְרֹאשׁ וְנוֹחַ לְתִשְׁחֹרֶת וֶהֱוֵי
מְקַבֵּל אֶת־כָּל־הָאָדָם בְּשִׂמְחָה:

יז רַבִּי עֲקִיבָה אוֹמֵר, שְׂחוֹק וְקַלּוּת רֹאשׁ מַרְגִּילִין אֶת־הָאָדָם
לְעֶרְוָה: מַסֹּרֶת סְיָג לַתּוֹרָה, מַעַשְׂרוֹת סְיָג לָעֹשֶׁר, נְדָרִים סְיָג
לַפְּרִישׁוּת, סְיָג לַחָכְמָה שְׁתִיקָה:

---

16. ראש here denotes a person who occupies the position of "head", of leadership, in an organization or in any endeavor. קל, literally, "easy to be led",
"amenable". נוח is "quiet", "cautious". תשחרת is "youth", the "morning" of
life, as in מרחם משחר (Psalm 110:31), and הילדות והשחרות (Eccl. 11:10). When
dealing with a person entrusted with the leadership of an assembly, a group
or a community to which you belong, be amenable. Do not be difficult, submit to his direction, and do not regard this submission as a loss of face. But
when you deal with the inexperienced young, be cautious. Give ample thought
to the matter at hand before making your decision. However once you find
that what they seek to achieve is good, then join them in their endeavors even
though they are younger than you. When other men offer you their help in
your own endeavors, accept them cheerfully. Do not be led by pride to seek to
do everything by yourself. Do not reject anyone from the outset; instead, receive
everyone gladly, and then consider whether or not he is suitable for you and
your endeavors. All these three verses urge that you selflessly ignore personal
factors in favor of pure devotion to the cause you seek to serve.

17. In moments of jest and levity we may permit ourselves to treat lightly
those things which are normally taken as seriously as they should be. By the
light treatment we give them at such moments we run the risk of having
sacred and solemn things lose their lofty and inviolable character for us and
thus, in fact, of drawing close to lewdness and unchastity, first in thought and
word and then, gradually, even in deed. —מסרת, the traditional text of the
Written Word of God guards the Scriptures against falsification; and the
traditional interpretation of the content of the Law protects the latter from
distortion. —מעשרות: The three tithes, מעשר שני ,מעשר ראשון, מעשר עני and
guard our riches against perverted use by teaching us the proper uses for
them and guiding us to the practical implementation of these teachings. The
maaser rishon, the tithe to be given to the Levites, teaches and accustoms us
to attend to the spiritual needs of our Torah knowledge and to the maintenance

16. Rabbi Yishmael said: Be amenable with a superior, cautious with the young, and receive all men with cheerfulness.

17. Rabbi Akiva said: Jesting and levity accustom a man to lewdness. The transmission is a protective fence about the Torah, the tithes are a fence for riches, vows are a fence for abstinence; a fence for wisdom is silence.

---

of the bearers and teachers of the Torah before seeking to gratify our own physical needs. The *maaser sheni*, the second tithe, which must be eaten in the environs of the Sanctuary in Jerusalem, teaches and accustoms us to make even our act of physical enjoyment so sacred that, thus elevated to the sphere of duty in the service of God, it need not shun even the presence of God and the environs of His sanctuary. The *maaser ani*, the tithe for the poor teaches and accustoms us to view the possessions given us by God as having been given us not only for ourselves, not only for our own physical nourishment and sustenance, but also as a means for giving aid and support to our less fortunate brethren. Thus we learn to regard ourselves as Divinely-appointed instruments and messengers of God's own bounty. But our sages teach us that while the *maaseroth* are thus fences guarding our riches against misuse, they serve, at the same time, to protect our wealth against decline. They teach us that עשר תעשר, עשר בשביל שתתעשר, tithing will make you rich; and in Malachi 3:10 we are told הביאו את כל המעשר וגו' "Bring all your tithes, etc.," ובחנוני נא בזאת וגו', "and thus put me to the test, to see whether I will not open the heavens for you and pour upon you blessings without an end." (Taanith 9a). — נדרים: God does not view the making of vows with favor; it is expected that we do good without first having to resort to vows to resolve to do so. Nevertheless, the vow is commended as a means for the exercise and the strengthening of our resolve to abstain from sin in the struggle against evil impulses. — סיג לחכמה שתיקה: Surely this does not mean "absolute silence". What is meant is that art of remaining silent practiced by him who would rather say nothing at all than deliver himself of a rash ill-considered statement, who listens quietly to the views of others in order to learn from them, and who does not have the urge to shine forth with his own opinions and to refuse to let others get in a word edgewise. Such a person will devote more time to thought than to speech and will therefore never run the danger of making any statement that is thoughtless or ill-considered.

יח הוּא הָיָה אוֹמֵר, חָבִיב אָדָם שֶׁנִּבְרָא בְּצֶלֶם · חִבָּה יְתֵרָה
נוֹדַעַת לוֹ שֶׁנִּבְרָא בְּצֶלֶם (אֱלֹהִים) שֶׁנֶּאֱמַר כִּי בְּצֶלֶם אֱלֹהִים
עָשָׂה אֶת־הָאָדָם: חֲבִיבִין יִשְׂרָאֵל שֶׁנִּקְרְאוּ בָנִים (לַמָּקוֹם)· חִבָּה
יְתֵרָה נוֹדַעַת לָהֶם שֶׁנִּקְרְאוּ בָנִים לַמָּקוֹם שֶׁנֶּאֱמַר בָּנִים אַתֶּם
לַיָי אֱלֹהֵיכֶם: חֲבִיבִין יִשְׂרָאֵל שֶׁנִּתַּן לָהֶם כְּלִי חֶמְדָּה· חִבָּה
יְתֵרָה נוֹדַעַת לָהֶם שֶׁנִּתַּן לָהֶם כְּלִי חֶמְדָּה שֶׁבּוֹ נִבְרָא הָעוֹלָם
שֶׁנֶּאֱמַר כִּי לֶקַח טוֹב נָתַתִּי לָכֶם תּוֹרָתִי אַל־תַּעֲזֹבוּ :

---

18. The Mishna here enumerates the privileges of which man was found worthy as distinguished from other creatures, and the special signs of Divine love by which Israel, in turn, was singled out from the rest of mankind. The fact that these distinctions were not given without the recipients' being made aware of them, is construed as an additional mark of Divine favor. Man was favored by having been created in the image of God. This in itself would be a wondrous gift, even if man would not be aware of it at all. For by virtue of the godly qualities with which he was thus endowed at the time of his creation he would do much that is morally and spiritually good, even though he would not be aware that by so conducting himself he was merely demonstrating his resemblance to God. But this special divine favor attained its full worth only by virtue of the fact that man was taught explicitly that his dignity and nobleness which raises him above all other creatures, and his destiny which guides him toward God in moral and spiritual perfection are based upon his having been created in the image of the Lord.—The divine favor accorded Israel as distinguished from all other men is that the relationship it enjoys with God is much closer than that of the rest of mankind. The tie which links God with Israel is like that which binds a father to his child. Even if God would simply have given Israel this special fatherly love, guidance and training, without Israel ever becoming aware of its special position and relationship to God, it would have been no mean favor. But actually, this token of God's love, too, shines forth in its true worth only by virtue of the fact that Israel was told of it and thus spurred on to hallowing self-respect and to childlike, loving obedience and childlike trust in God. Accompanying this favor of being called "the children of God", and, in fact, its true purpose and goal, is the other great privilege accorded Israel—its

18. He used to say: Privileged is man, for he was created in His image. But it was an act of special favor that it was made known to him that he was created in His image, as it is said: "For in the image of God did He create man." Privileged are Yisrael, for they are called children. But it was an act of special favor that it was made known to them that they are called the children of God; for it is said: "You are children to *God* your God." Privileged are Yisrael, for a precious instrument was given them through which the world was created, for it is said: "I have given you a teaching that is suited to the good; forsake not My Torah."

---

appointment as bearer of the Torah. Even if Israel were merely to accept the contents of the Torah as a God-given guide to moral and spiritual perfection and the fulfillment of its life's task, if it were to live for its realization with the unreserved devotion of all its being, its thoughts, and its efforts, all without having been told of the unique and sacred significance of the Torah for the whole world, this Divine appointment would have been a priceless privilege. But God explicitly made His people aware of the fact that the Torah was a כלי חמדה, literally "an instrument with which to strive after the goal" through which and for the sake of which the whole world was made. The laws of the Torah are those laws by which all the creatures, phenomena, and developments of all the rest of creation continue and endure, transposed into a smaller scale to be a law for the shaping of the lives of individuals and nations. At the same time the Torah is the instrument for the fulfillment of that goal for which the Lord created the whole world to begin with. The purpose and the goal of the physical world is טוב, the realization of all that is morally good; the verdict of *tov* was pronounced over the work of every single day of creation and finally over the sum total of the Universe that was thus brought into being. But this "good", the goal for which the entire world was made and which it is man's task to achieve, can be attained only through the Torah. The Torah is לקח טוב; it is a teaching through which the good can be won. Therefore God warns us: תורתי אל תעזבו. Thus our awareness of the unique and lofty significance of the Torah should help us view the Torah as that inalienable good for whose preservation, realization and ever-increasing acknowledgement we should live, offering up to its fulfillment all that we are and all that we have, and, if need be, even life itself.

יט הַכֹּל צָפוּי וְהָרְשׁוּת נְתוּנָה· וּבְטוֹב הָעוֹלָם נָדוֹן · וְהַכֹּל לְפִי רֹב הַמַּעֲשֶׂה:

כ הוּא הָיָה אוֹמֵר, הַכֹּל נָתוּן בָּעֵרָבוֹן· וּמְצוּדָה פְרוּשָׂה עַל־כָּל־הַחַיִּים· הֶחָנוּת פְּתוּחָה וְהַחֶנְוָנִי מַקִּיף· וְהַפִּנְקָס פָּתוּחַ וְהַיָּד כּוֹתֶבֶת· וְכָל הָרוֹצֶה לִלְווֹת יָבֹא וְיִלְוֶה · וְהַגַּבָּאִין מַחֲזִירִין תָּדִיר בְּכָל־יוֹם וְנִפְרָעִין מִן הָאָדָם מִדַּעְתּוֹ וְשֶׁלֹּא מִדַּעְתּוֹ וְיֵשׁ לָהֶם עַל מַה שֶׁיִּסְמֹכוּ· וְהַדִּין דִּין אֱמֶת וְהַכֹּל מְתֻקָּן לִסְעוּדָה:

כא רַבִּי אֶלְעָזָר בֶּן עֲזַרְיָה אוֹמֵר· אִם אֵין תּוֹרָה אֵין דֶּרֶךְ אֶרֶץ, אִם אֵין דֶּרֶךְ אֶרֶץ אֵין תּוֹרָה· אִם אֵין חָכְמָה אֵין יִרְאָה, אִם אֵין יִרְאָה אֵין חָכְמָה· אִם אֵין דַּעַת אֵין בִּינָה, אִם אֵין בִּינָה אֵין דַּעַת· אִם אֵין קֶמַח אֵין תּוֹרָה, אִם אֵין תּוֹרָה אֵין קֶמַח:

19. When God first made the world and put man into it, He foresaw that man could do both good and evil. Therefore He ordered the world in such a manner that the evil done by man would not thwart the goal of His world sovereignty but that, instead, even the evil that would be done by man would prove an instrument for the good in the end, although those who did it would never know and never have intended that this should be so. Man has been given the freedom of choice. In fact, if it were not within man's power to do evil, were sin to hold no charms for him, indeed, man would then not be human at all. His virtue would be no virtue, and all of his actions would be on a level no higher than animal instinct. And the world is judged in accordance with the good that is done in it. In His reign over the world God sees to it that the good, of which we have seen a beginning even now among men, is not suppressed or choked off by the weed of evil. And He so guides the course of time that the good which exists will not be lost but, instead, gain ground and spread steadily, and in the end spring into full bloom as a kingdom of the good on earth. But the gauge with which any one period of time will be measured, and by which its fate will be determined, will be the nature, good or bad, of the majority of that which has come to pass and still comes to pass through the deeds of men.

20. Everything that has been given us by God imposes an obligation upon us, and whatever we are and whatever we possess constitutes the pledge for the discharge of our debt. No man can escape either this obligation or the attachment of this pledge. We all have the freedom to choose whether to

19. Everything is foreseen, yet freedom [of choice] is given, and the world is judged according to the good, and the judgment of all is according to the nature of the majority of the events that have come to pass.

20. He used to say: Everything is given on pledge and a net is spread out over all the living. The shop is open, the merchant extends credit, the ledger is open and the hand records [therein]. Whosoever wishes to borrow—let him come and borrow. The collectors make their appointed round each day and take payment from man whether he knows it or not. It is on hand, that on which they can rely; the legal procedure is right. But all is ready for the festive banquet.

21. Rabbi Elazar ben Azariah, said: Where there is no Torah, there is no civic society; if there is no civic society, there is no Torah. Where there is no wisdom, there is no fear of God; where there is no fear of God, there is no wisdom. Where there is no knowledge, there is no understanding; where there is no understanding there is no knowledge. Where there is no sustenance there is no Torah; where there is no Torah there is no sustenance.

---

limit our debt by a life of moderation, or whether to increase it by lack of restraint. But we must remember at all times that no unpaid debt is ever cancelled. Even if we should forget about it, God will exact payment in His own way, whether we know of it or not. No one is pressed for payment, for the pledges are valid security, available at all times, and the procedure of redemption is in strict accordance with truth and justice. But even as payment is exacted for every neglect of duty, so rich reward await those who have remained steadfastly loyal to their task.

21. Without the Torah, without the spiritual guidance and moral ennoblement communicated by the Teaching of God, any endeavor to establish, maintain and advance a civilized society on earth will be in vain. Conversely, without דרך ארץ, if an orderly way of life is not fostered, then the guidance and ennoblement inherent in the Torah lack a foundation on earth. In that case the understanding for a great many situations covered by the Torah's teachings will be lost, as will be just as great a part of its practical application to daily living. Without חכמה, without the spiritual enlightenment to be derived from the Torah of God, the fear of God will not be properly realized or applied without error. Conversely, without יראה, without the fear of God, the endeavor to gather wisdom from the Torah is deprived of its basic prerequisite and motivation. Without דעת, without the knowledge of the nature and reality of things and circumstances, בינה, understanding, the good sense

כב הוּא הָיָה אוֹמֵר, כָּל שֶׁחָכְמָתוֹ מְרֻבָּה מִמַּעֲשָׂיו לְמָה הוּא
דוֹמֶה, לְאִילָן שֶׁעֲנָפָיו מְרֻבִּין וְשָׁרָשָׁיו מֻעָטִין וְהָרוּחַ בָּאָה
וְעוֹקַרְתּוּ וְהוֹפַכְתּוּ עַל פָּנָיו· שֶׁנֶּאֱמַר וְהָיָה כְּעַרְעָר בָּעֲרָבָה וְלֹא
יִרְאֶה כִּי יָבוֹא טוֹב וְשָׁכַן חֲרֵרִים בַּמִּדְבָּר אֶרֶץ מְלֵחָה וְלֹא תֵשֵׁב·
אֲבָל כָּל שֶׁמַּעֲשָׂיו מְרֻבִּים מֵחָכְמָתוֹ לְמָה הוּא דוֹמֶה, לְאִילָן
שֶׁעֲנָפָיו מֻעָטִין וְשָׁרָשָׁיו מְרֻבִּין שֶׁאֲפִילוּ כָּל הָרוּחוֹת שֶׁבָּעוֹלָם
בָּאוֹת וְנוֹשְׁבוֹת בּוֹ אֵין מְזִיזִין אוֹתוֹ מִמְּקוֹמוֹ, שֶׁנֶּאֱמַר וְהָיָה כְּעֵץ
שָׁתוּל עַל מַיִם וְעַל יוּבַל יְשַׁלַּח שָׁרָשָׁיו וְלֹא יִרְאֶה כִּי יָבֹא חֹם
וְהָיָה עָלֵהוּ רַעֲנָן וּבִשְׁנַת בַּצֹּרֶת לֹא יִדְאָג וְלֹא יָמִישׁ מֵעֲשׂוֹת
פֶּרִי :

כג רַבִּי אֶלְעָזָר (בֶּן־) חִסְמָא אוֹמֵר, קִנִּין וּפִתְחֵי נִדָּה הֵן הֵן
גּוּפֵי הֲלָכוֹת· תְּקוּפוֹת וְגִמַטְרִיָאוֹת פַּרְפְּרָאוֹת לַחָכְמָה:
רבי חנניא וכו׳· קדיש·

---

to be employed in making judgments, and in drawing inferences and conclusions, lacks a factual basis and will dissipate itself in false and unreal imagin-
ings. But conversely, without that "good sense" with which to test, evaluate,
and draw conclusions, *Daath,* that part of intelligence which constitutes knowledge, may go astray; it will take appearance for reality and will have no
protection against error and deception. Without *kemach,* without sustenance,
neither the study nor the dissemination of the Torah can be promoted. Conversely, without the Torah, without earnest attention to the moral and spiritual
"sustenance" to be derived through the Torah, the search after purely physical
sustenance not only loses all true worth and significance but actually is
destroyed by the outgrowths of crude materialism.

22. He used to say: He whose wisdom exceeds his deeds is like a tree whose branches are many but whose roots are few. The wind comes and uproots it and overturns it upon its top. Of such a man it is said: "He shall be like a lonely man in the wasteland and shall not see when good comes; he shall dwell upon the parched soil in the wilderness, a salt-saturated land which is uninhabitable." But he whose deeds exceed his wisdom is like a tree whose branches are few but whose roots are many. Even if all the winds of the world come and blow upon it, they cannot move it from its place. Of such a man it is said: "He shall be like a tree planted by the waters, which spreads out its roots to the stream of water; he shall not perceive it when the heat comes, but his leaf shall remain fresh; he will not be troubled in the year of drought, neither will he cease to bear fruit."

23. Rabbi Elazar ben Chisma, said: The chapters pertinent to the bird sacrifices and to the beginnings of woman's unclean period are important ordinances of the Law. Astronomy and geometry are condiments to wisdom.

---

22. Only such wisdom as is proven in practical action can endure and will in turn sustain him who is blessed with it. It is not extensive knowledge but only the knowledge that he has done good deeds in abundance that will steel a man against all trials and temptations, and will gain for him the protection and aid inherent in Divine approval.

23. קנין (Tractate Kinin in *Seder Kodshim*) and פתחי נדה (Arachin 8a) are stressed here solely as illustrations of treatises that serve to advance the conscientious fulfillment of our duty and bear resemblance to תקופות and גמטריות only insofar as they, too, involve calculations. פרפראות are "condiments" or "auxiliary sciences". Rabbi Eleazar Chisma was himself a mathematician of such renown that it was hyperbolically said of him that he knew how to determine the number of drops of water contained in the ocean. (Horioth 10a).

כל ישראל וכו'.

א בֶּן־זוֹמָא אוֹמֵר, אֵיזֶהוּ חָכָם, הַלּוֹמֵד מִכָּל־אָדָם שֶׁנֶּאֱמַר
מִכָּל־מְלַמְּדַי הִשְׂכַּלְתִּי (כִּי עֵדְוֹתֶיךָ שִׂיחָה לִי): אֵיזֶהוּ גִבּוֹר,
הַכּוֹבֵשׁ אֶת־יִצְרוֹ שֶׁנֶּאֱמַר טוֹב אֶרֶךְ אַפַּיִם מִגִּבּוֹר וּמֹשֵׁל בְּרוּחוֹ
מִלֹּכֵד עִיר: אֵיזֶהוּ עָשִׁיר, הַשָּׂמֵחַ בְּחֶלְקוֹ שֶׁנֶּאֱמַר יְגִיעַ כַּפֶּיךָ כִּי
תֹאכֵל אַשְׁרֶיךָ וְטוֹב לָךְ · אַשְׁרֶיךָ בָּעוֹלָם הַזֶּה וְטוֹב לָךְ לָעוֹלָם
הַבָּא: אֵיזֶהוּ מְכֻבָּד, הַמְכַבֵּד אֶת־הַבְּרִיּוֹת שֶׁנֶּאֱמַר כִּי מְכַבְּדַי
אֲכַבֵּד וּבֹזַי יֵקָלּוּ:

---

1. According to these "Ethics of the Fathers" it is primarily the knowledge of the Torah that stamps a person as a חכם. This Godly teaching contains nothing that is supernatural or other-worldly. Indeed, it is the purpose of the Torah of God to shape and regulate in every detail every single one of the manifold aspects and relationships of practical life on earth. It therefore deals in exhaustive detail with all the immediate things of the here and now. The basic prerequisite for the proper fulfillment of the laws of God is knowledge, as extensive as possible, of the realities of all earthly, human relationships; a vast and varied store of wisdom such as has been amassed and left to us by our sages in sciences such as agriculture, cattle breeding, industry, commerce, pharmacology, and nutrition, to name but a few. In view of the foregoing, the true *talmid chacham* will find that he can learn something from every person with whom he speaks, for any person can be more expert than he in at least one calling or pursuit and thus can give him valuable practical information which he may then utilize for his study of the Law of God. For the laws of the Torah are not simply עֵדוּת, "testimonies" of God; they are also עֵדוּת, "ornaments" designed to impress upon all human affairs the stamp of the morally good and beautiful.

איזהו גבור. Even the mightiest hero may fall victim to the pull of his passion. Therefore he who can subdue his passions is mightier than the bravest of warriors.

The greed for physical pleasure is circumscribed by gratification and satiation. But the striving after money, the *means* for pleasure, has no limit for though money in itself does not give pleasure, it makes possible all future enjoyment. Therefore the lust for money can never be satisfied. And a man's craving for more and more wealth may well grow to such excess that the

1. Ben Zoma said: Who is wise? He who learns from all men. For it is said: "From all those who have taught me I have gotten understanding, for Your ennobling testimonies are my pursuits." Who is strong? He who subdues his passions. For it is said: "He who is slow to anger is better than a hero, and he who has control over his will is better than he who conquers a city." Who is rich? He who rejoices in his portion. For it is said: "When you enjoy the work of your hands, then you shall stride forward and it shall be well with you." Progress in this world and good in the world to come. Who is honored? He who honors others. For it is said: "For those who honor Me I will honor and those who despise Me shall be held in contempt."

---

lack of what he does not now possess may actually mar his joy in whatever he does have at present. Yet it is precisely this joy in what one possesses, this contentment with one's portion that constitutes the only genuine treasure and the sole true happiness in life; without it, even the richest of men will remain poor in the midst of all his wealth. Hence the surest way not only to become rich but also to remain so is to limit one's wishes to the modest measure of that which is necessary and within reach, and above all, to learn to view חלקי, whatever God has given one, with rejoicing, as the "portion" granted him by Heaven to be utilized for the discharge of his task on earth. This awareness of where one's duty lies can endow any God-given "portion" with irreplaceable, infinitely blissful worth.* Desire no more than you have— and you are indeed rich.

איזהו מכובד. It is the most common thing that people who seek honor for themselves behave toward others with reserve bordering on arrogance, and that they make very much of themselves but very little of others. Such conduct, they think, is the surest way to secure the respect and esteem of others. But this Mishna knows otherwise. Honor, genuine honor, is just another one of the gifts deriving from God, and it has a way of going to him who covets it least. He who does not despise any of his fellowmen, but respects them all as בריות, as "creations" of God, giving them due honor for the sake of Him Who created them, actually honors God, the Creator of them all. And of such a man, God says, "Him who honors Me, I shall honor." Conversely, he who despises his fellow-men God will let sink into oblivion.

---

* The German term "reich" is appropriate: Rich ("reich") is he who has achieved ("erreicht") what he wants.

ב בֶּן־עַזַּאי אוֹמֵר, הֱוֵי רָץ לְמִצְוָה קַלָּה וּבוֹרֵחַ מִן־הָעֲבֵרָה, שֶׁמִּצְוָה גוֹרֶרֶת מִצְוָה וַעֲבֵרָה גוֹרֶרֶת עֲבֵרָה שֶׁשְּׂכַר מִצְוָה מִצְוָה וּשְׂכַר עֲבֵרָה עֲבֵרָה:

ג הוּא הָיָה אוֹמֵר, אַל־תְּהִי בָז לְכָל־אָדָם וְאַל־תְּהִי מַפְלִיג לְכָל־דָּבָר שֶׁאֵין לְךָ אָדָם שֶׁאֵין לוֹ שָׁעָה וְאֵין לְךָ דָּבָר שֶׁאֵין לוֹ מָקוֹם:

ד רַבִּי לְוִיטַס אִישׁ יַבְנֶה אוֹמֵר, מְאֹד מְאֹד הֱוֵי שְׁפַל רוּחַ שֶׁתִּקְוַת אֱנוֹשׁ רִמָּה:

ה רַבִּי יוֹחָנָן בֶּן־בְּרוֹקָה אוֹמֵר, כָּל־הַמְחַלֵּל שֵׁם שָׁמַיִם בְּסֵתֶר נִפְרָעִין מִמֶּנּוּ בַּגָּלוּי. אֶחָד שׁוֹגֵג וְאֶחָד מֵזִיד בְּחִלּוּל הַשֵּׁם:

2. Should you have an opportunity to perform a *Mitzvah,* do not let it pass by; perhaps the *Mitzvah* seems so easy that you might think there would be ample opportunity to do it at other times; or perhaps, since it appears to be so simple, it may seem to you so trifling as to make you think that even failure to perform it would not hurt your conscience overmuch. Yet, let nothing deter you from fulfilling it, for you cannot afford to overlook the consequences, both seen and unseen, of any *Mitzvah.* The good that you do will lead to more good, and every act of duty done bears its own reward. The knowledge that you have done the will of your Father in Heaven will bring you closer to Him; it will enrich your spirit with the happy awareness of having done the right thing, and reinforce your moral capacity for doing good. The reverse is true of sin. Do not underestimate the consequences of even the most trivial wrong. It is not enough merely not to sin in action; Flee far from evil and shun anything that might lead to it. For you can foresee neither the effect nor sequel of a sin. Evil leads to more evil, and every sin bears within itself the seeds of its own punishment. It removes you from the pure and loving Presence of your Father in Heaven; it will awaken within you the torturing pangs of conscience, it will dull the keen edge of your moral judgement and weaken your resistance to future evil.

3. There is no such person or thing that cannot be of serious harm or, conversely, of great profit to you at some future time. Therefore it behooves you never to despise any person or any thing.

4. It would seem probable that this statement derives from the view that all arrogance and all prideful presumption are rooted in the sensuous physical aspects of the human personality. The purely spiritual and moral forces within

2. Ben Azzai said: Hasten to do even the slightest *Mitzvah* and flee from all sin, for one *Mitzvah* will lead to another *Mitzvah,* and one sin to another sin, for the recompense of a *Mitzvah* is inherent in the *Mitzvah,* while the recompense of sin is the sin.

3. He used to say: Despise not any man and do not deem anything unworthy of consideration, for there is no man that does not have his hour and no thing that does not have its place.

4. Rabbi Levitas of Yavneh said: Be exceedingly humble in spirit, for the hope of earthly man is but decay.

5. Rabbi Yochanan ben Berokah, said: He who profanes the Name of God in secret will suffer the penalty of being unmasked in public. This is true regardless of whether the *Chillul Hashem* is perpetrated in error or intentionally.

---

us make for modesty as a matter of course, for they are so deeply imbued with the magnitude of the task at hand that whatever we may have achieved or accomplished needs must fade ino utter insignificance when compared to the vastness of the task to be fulfilled. Therefore it is appropriate to admonish the proud and the arrogant to remember that all those aspirations that depend on the realm of the physical and sensual can end only in decay.

5. חלול השם is deemed the most serious of all transgressions. It is that sin which is perpetrated when a person who is qualified, by virtue of his calling or station, to teach and, both by word and by personal example, to champion and promote among men the hallowing of God's Name and the conscientious fulfillment of His Law, publicly shows contempt for the Name of God and openly transgresses the command of His will. We are told here that, even if such a man feigns dutiful loyalty in public and leads a sinful life in private only, he will suffer the punishment of being exposed in public for what he really is so that all may behold his unworthiness. — אחד שוגג any error in the sphere of the fulfillment of life's duty betokens a lack of understanding, caution and circumspection in this aspect of living, and also a certain degree of indifference to the concept of loyalty properly due to the Law of God. Therefore, any error committed in this connection by one to whom men look up in admiration as an example for themselves to emulate, has an adverse influence upon the attitude that should by right be adopted by his fellow men. This is true even if it was obvious to all that the act committed had been an error. And the fact is that, all too often, such acts are not always or by all recognized as errors and thus one error may persist in memory as a dangerous example set by a man whom others seek to emulate. For this reason it is not enough that a person to whom others look as a model by which to guide their own conduct should take more than ordinary care to keep from sinning on

י רַבִּי יִשְׁמָעֵאל בַּר רַבִּי יוֹסֵי אוֹמֵר, הַלּוֹמֵד עַל־מְנָת לְלַמֵּד מַסְפִּיקִים בְּיָדוֹ לִלְמוֹד וּלְלַמֵּד וְהַלּוֹמֵד עַל־מְנָת לַעֲשׂוֹת מַסְפִּיקִים בְּיָדוֹ לִלְמוֹד וּלְלַמֵּד לִשְׁמוֹר וְלַעֲשׂוֹת:

יא רַבִּי צָדוֹק אוֹמֵר, אַל־(תִּפְרוֹשׁ מִן־הַצִּבּוּר וְאַל־)תַּעַשׂ עַצְמָךְ כְּעוֹרְכֵי הַדַּיָּנִין וְאַל־)תַּעֲשֶׂהָ עֲטָרָה לְהִתְגַּדֵּל־בָּהּ וְלֹא קַרְדּוֹם לַחְפָּר־בָּהּ. וְכָךְ הָיָה הִלֵּל אוֹמֵר וּדְאִשְׁתַּמַּשׁ בְּתַגָּא חֲלָף, הָא לָמַדְתָּ כָּל־הַנֶּהֱנֶה מִדִּבְרֵי תוֹרָה נוֹטֵל חַיָּיו מִן־הָעוֹלָם:

יב רַבִּי יוֹסֵי אוֹמֵר, כָּל־הַמְכַבֵּד אֶת־הַתּוֹרָה גּוּפוֹ מְכֻבָּד עַל־הַבְּרִיּוֹת וְכָל־הַמְחַלֵּל אֶת־הַתּוֹרָה גּוּפוֹ מְחֻלָּל עַל־הַבְּרִיּוֹת:

---

purpose; it is required of him that he must be carefully on his guard to avoid doing such wrongs even unwittingly or in error.

6. Quite aside from its predominant *Mitzvah* value, the intention to pass on, by means of instruction, that which one has learned, is itself conducive to study, for the one who studies for this purpose is thus compelled to delve even more thoroughly into the material to be learned and to seek greater clarity of thought than he might otherwise. But the supreme purpose of learning Torah is to translate the teaching of the Word of God into practical deeds in loyal fulfillment thereof. This purpose embraces not only the duty to act in this manner, but also that of teaching the Word of God to everyone who is needful of such instruction and capable of grasping it. Quite aside from the all-important *Mitzvah* value inherent in this act, the very intention and resolve to fulfill that which is to be learned is at the same time that attitude which is most conducive to proper study. To discern, from the Word of the Law, the will of God as regards the arrangement of our own lives requires the clearest, broadest and most profound penetration and understanding of the Torah. But over and beyond even this, that laudable intention is in itself inimical to any erroneous view, be it ever so ingenious, that may corrupt the mind with its wit and casuistry; and it will ever keep before us the reminder that "any error in theoretical study will lead to wrongdoing in practice."— שִׁגְגַת תַּלְמוּד עוֹלָה זָדוֹן.

7. It is not through the individual, but through the community and through the congregation which represent that community on a smaller scale, that Judaism lives on forever. Besides, it was not the Jewish individual but the *Kehilath Yaakov*, the Jewish community that God appointed as the bearer

6. Rabbi Yishmael ben Rabbi Yosé said: To him who learns in order to teach, Heaven will grant the opportunity both to learn and to teach; but to him who learns in order to practice, Heaven will grant the opportunity to learn and to teach, to guard and to practice.

7. Rabbi Tzadok said: Do not set yourself apart from the community and act not as the counsel of the judges. Make not of it [the Torah] a crown with which to aggrandize yourself, nor an axe with which to strike. Thus said Hillel: "He who makes use of the crown [of the Torah] shall pass away." Thence you may learn that he who derives selfish gain from the words of the Torah thereby takes his own life away from this world.

8. Rabbi Yosé said: He who honors the Torah will himself be honored by mankind, but he who dishonors the Torah will himself be disdained by mankind.

---

of His sacred cause. Therefore the Jewish individual can fulfill his true purpose only in communion with the congregation, and accordingly he is earnestly admonished not to separate himself from the congregation, but to cleave to it in both joy and sorrow, to share its burdens and to help it discharge its tasks. However, it is self-understood that this duty exists only so long as the congregation, in its turn, will not forsake the inalienable eternal destiny of the Jewish community and thus, in fact, cease to be Jewish. Once that should happen, then the course to be taken by the individual is equally clear and unequivocal. He must then abide by the ruling: לא תהיה אחרי רבים לרעות which tells us not to follow the majority on the path of evil. — אל תעש וכו׳ (see Chap. 1:8). — אל תעשה וכו׳. Do not debase the wisdom of the Word of God to use it as a tool for self-aggrandizement or selfish gain. The sacred wisdom is a crown of which it is written כי הוא חייכם "The Word of God is your very life." He who debases the Torah violates it and therefore brings about his own destruction. — וכך היה הלל אומר (see Chap. 1:13)

8. He who accepts the Torah as the sole, supreme source of truth and of guiding human purpose will receive from the Torah in turn that spiritual stature and moral ennoblement which will earn him the honor and respect of his fellow-men without his having to seek such recognition. But he who will deny the Torah the honor and respect due it and will not permit the Torah to bring its spiritual and moral influence to bear upon his thoughts and endeavors will descend to a level of base worthlessness and will have to forego all hope of ever receiving the esteem and respect of others.

ט רַבִּי יִשְׁמָעֵאל בְּנוֹ אוֹמֵר, הַחוֹשֵׂךְ עַצְמוֹ מִן־הַדִּין פּוֹרֵק
מִמֶּנּוּ אֵיבָה וְגָזֵל וּשְׁבוּעַת שָׁוְא, וְהַגַּס לִבּוֹ בְּהוֹרָאָה שׁוֹטֶה רָשָׁע
וְגַס רוּחַ:

י הוּא הָיָה אוֹמֵר, אַל־תְּהִי דָן יְחִידִי שֶׁאֵין דָּן יְחִידִי אֶלָּא אֶחָד,
וְאַל־תֹּאמַר קַבְּלוּ דַעְתִּי שֶׁהֵם רַשָּׁאִים וְלֹא אָתָּה:

יא רַבִּי יוֹנָתָן אוֹמֵר, כָּל־הַמְקַיֵּם אֶת־הַתּוֹרָה מֵעֹנִי סוֹפוֹ לְקַיְּמָהּ
מֵעֹשֶׁר· וְכָל־הַמְבַטֵּל אֶת־הַתּוֹרָה מֵעֹשֶׁר סוֹפוֹ לְבַטְּלָהּ מֵעֹנִי:

יב רַבִּי מֵאִיר אוֹמֵר, הֱוֵי מְמַעֵט בְּעֵסֶק וַעֲסֹק בַּתּוֹרָה וֶהֱוֵה
שְׁפַל־רוּחַ בִּפְנֵי כָל־אָדָם וְאִם־בָּטַלְתָּ מִן־הַתּוֹרָה יֶשׁ־לְךָ בְּטֵלִים
הַרְבֵּה כְּנֶגְדֶּךָ וְאִם־עָמַלְתָּ בַתּוֹרָה יֶשׁ־לוֹ שָׂכָר הַרְבֵּה לִתֶּן־לָךְ:

9. If there is another properly qualified person available to administer justice, it is the part of wisdom to decline the function of judge or arbitrator. For, though he may have made his decision in strict accordance with the dictates of his conscience, the judge as a rule incurs the hostility of the losing party. Besides, even with best of intentions and after the most conscientious deliberation, a judge is still not immune to error and may thus, albeit unintentionally, perpetrate a miscarriage of justice and wrongfully deprive one party of its just due. Finally, most of the cases where sworn testimony is required, involve either שבועת שקר, outright perjury, or else, in instances where he against whom the testimony is made, is convinced of the truth of that testimony even without a sworn deposition, שבועת שוא, an oath taken in vain. It is true that, in cases where he is the only one fit to administer justice, the person filling the function of judge has carried out a most important duty. In fact, in the Hebrew language a conscientious judge is called by the name of God Himself, אלקים, implying that he acts as a representative of God on earth. But by the same token he who is not compelled to act in this capacity is spared a responsibility that is certainly not to be taken lightly. Of course he who impudently seeks to force his own decision upon others only exposes thereby his deficiency in wisdom and scruples, as well as his foolish conceit.

10. Even though any man of recognized faithfulness to the law (מומחה לרבים) is permitted to act as a judge without associates, it is advisable that he refrain from doing so. For only God, the sole Judge with Whom error is impossible, should judge alone. If you should be a member of a tribunal of judges, do not insist on your own views. For in any tribunal it is only the majority of the judges, rather than any single one among them, that has the authority to make the decision.

9. Rabbi Yishmael, his son, said: He who shuns judicial office rids himself of hatred, robbery and perjury. But he who presumptuously lays down decisions on the law is foolish, lawless and arrogant.

10. He used to say: Judge not alone, for there is only One Who may judge alone. And say not, "Accept my view," for it is they and not you that have the authority.

11. Rabbi Yonathan says: He who fulfills the Torah out of poverty shall also fulfill it out of wealth; he who neglects the Torah out of wealth shall also neglect it out of poverty.

12. Rabbi Meir says: Limit your business activities and occupy yourself with the Torah instead, and be of humble spirit before all men. If you should neglect the Torah you will have to compete with many [others] who neglect the Torah, but if you toil in the Torah, God has abundant recompense to give you.

---

11. He whom the lack of material wealth, joys and pleasures will bring only nearer to the Torah, to that eternally inalienable, ever-present source of all moral and spiritual riches, bliss, and joy, and who finds in the Torah ample compensation for the things he must do without,—he will observe the Torah even if his circumstances should improve. Even if his material wealth should increase, he will still proudly cleave to the faithful study and observance of the Torah which alone endows earthly wealth with true and genuine worth. The greater the treasures he may acquire, the more will he devote them to the effort the better to discharge his God-given task. Not so he whom the superabundance of material possessions and pleasures makes insensitive and impervious to those moral and spiritual values that can be derived only from the faithful study and observance of the Torah. If his wealth in earthly goods should ever crumble, he will be so utterly absorbed in desperate attempts to recoup his lost fortune that he will have neither the wish, nor, he thinks, the time, to seek the way to that wealth and to that happiness which changes on earth cannot affect, and which can be found only in the study and observance of the Laws of the Torah.

12. Do a little less business so that you may gain additional time to engage in the study of the Torah. The financial sacrifice involved will be easier for you if you will accustom yourself to a more modest standard of living in the social circles in which you move. Remember that if, in order not to lag behind in other endeavors, you deprive the Torah of its rightful place in your life, you will have chosen a path upon which you will have many competitors to contend with, men who, like you, have neglected the Torah in order to devote their energies to the race for selfish gain. At the same time, bear in mind that the Lord has ample recompense in store for him who foregoes all other gain in order to toil upon the field of the Torah.

יג רַבִּי אֱלִיעֶזֶר בֶּן־יַעֲקֹב אוֹמֵר, הָעוֹשֶׂה מִצְוָה אַחַת קוֹנֶה
לוֹ פְּרַקְלִיט אֶחָד וְהָעוֹבֵר עֲבֵרָה אַחַת קוֹנֶה לוֹ קַטֵּגוֹר אֶחָד,
תְּשׁוּבָה וּמַעֲשִׂים טוֹבִים כִּתְרֵיס בִּפְנֵי הַפּוּרְעָנוּת:

יד רַבִּי יוֹחָנָן הַסַּנְדְּלָר אוֹמֵר, כָּל־כְּנֵסִיָּה שֶׁהִיא לְשֵׁם שָׁמַיִם
סוֹפָהּ לְהִתְקַיֵּם וְשֶׁאֵינָהּ לְשֵׁם שָׁמַיִם אֵין סוֹפָהּ לְהִתְקַיֵּם:

טו רַבִּי אֶלְעָזָר בֶּן שַׁמּוּעַ אוֹמֵר, יְהִי כְבוֹד תַּלְמִידְךָ חָבִיב עָלֶיךָ
כְּשֶׁלָּךְ וּכְבוֹד חֲבֵרְךָ כְּמוֹרָא רַבָּךְ וּמוֹרָא רַבָּךְ כְּמוֹרָא
שָׁמַיִם :

טז רַבִּי יְהוּדָה אוֹמֵר, הֱוֵה זָהִיר בְּתַלְמוּד שֶׁשִּׁגְגַת תַּלְמוּד
עוֹלָה זָדוֹן :

יז רַבִּי שִׁמְעוֹן אוֹמֵר, שְׁלֹשָׁה כְתָרִים הֵן· כֶּתֶר תּוֹרָה וְכֶתֶר
כְּהֻנָּה וְכֶתֶר מַלְכוּת·וְכֶתֶר שֵׁם טוֹב עוֹלֶה עַל גַּבֵּיהֶן:

13. Our happiness in both this world and the next depends upon our conduct
as regards our duty. Every *Mitzvah* we fulfill will be one more advocate
before God to speak in our behalf, while every sin we commit will stand as
one more accuser to testify against us before Him who guides our destinies.
Constant endeavor to become better and good deeds serve as protective armors
against any calamity.

14. The term לשם שמים describes any endeavor for the promotion of a good
thing for its own sake, without any ulterior motive. As Abrabanel notes in
connection with this Mishna, any organization so conceived bears within itself
the prerequisite for permanent endurance by virtue of the fact that its members all bear allegiance to its good cause and will subordinate all personal
interests to this their common goal. But in an organization based on ignoble
motives the members will soon be led to dicker with one another over personal
interests, and such rivalry bears within it the seed of sure disintegration which
will then be only a matter of time.

15. The subject of discussion here is not the extent to which the honor of
one's student should be protected, nor the degree of reverence due to a teacher
or to God Himself. What is brought out here is simply the fact that honor
is due even to our pupils and disciples and that we are duty bound to protect
it; and that we are not to violate the reverence due our teachers and our God.
When teaching our students and in our dealings with them we must never

13.   Rabbi Eliezer ben Yaakov, said: He who fulfills one commandment gains for himself one advocate; and he who commits one sin acquires for himself one accuser [thereby]. Repentance and good deeds are a shield against calamity.

14.   Rabbi Yochanan Ha-Sandlar said: Every assembly out of pure motives for the promotion of noble purposes will in the end endure, but that which is not out of pure motives and for noble purposes will in the end not endure.

15.   Rabbi Elazar ben Shamua, said: Let the honor of your student be as dear to you as your own; let the honor of your friend be as dear to you as the reverence due your teacher; and let the reverence due your teacher be as dear to you as the reverence due to Heaven.

16.   Rabbi Yehuda said: Be cautious in study, for an error in study amounts to intentional sin.

17.   Rabbi Shimon said: There are three crowns; the crown of the Torah, the crown of priesthood and the crown of kingship. But the crown of a good name excels them all.

---

allow ourselves, in our zeal to teach and discipline, to degrade or injure the dignity of a disciple. When associating with our equals on a more familiar footing, we must not let intimacy lead us to forget for one moment the deference with which we must treat their honor. Finally, any violation on our part of the reverence we owe to our teachers should weigh upon our conscience as heavily as would any act of irreverence against God Himself.

16.   The neglect, or the improper or superficial study of our Torah in theory will give rise to error and sin in practice. Our sin may be due to error only, but if that error results from indifference to the knowledge of our duty, and from intentional failure to seek better guidance by studying our Torah, then, in view of the indifference and intentional neglect that is at its cause, the error, though unintentional in itself, becomes a sin subject to punishment. Thus we read in Lev. 17:21 פשעיהם לכל חטאתם (see Commentary ibid.).

17.   The "crown of a good name" excels the other three, first by virtue of the fact that it is within the reach of all, without exception, and secondly because all the other three are without value unless they are linked with the crown of a good name. Any of these three crowns can be truly "crowns" only if he who wears them is deserving also of the crown of a good name because he shines forth both as a human being and as a Jew, distinguished in moral purity and devotion to duty, and particularly in the exemplary fulfillment of those duties and those opportunities to do good that are connected with the station of honor and privilege he occupies. It may also be that עולה על גביהן means [that the "crown of a good name]...must be linked with them all."

יח רַבִּי נְהוֹרָאי אוֹמֵר, הֱוֵי גוֹלֶה לִמְקוֹם תּוֹרָה, וְאַל־תֹּאמַר שֶׁהִיא תָבוֹא אַחֲרֶיךָ שֶׁחֲבֵרֶיךָ יְקַיְּמוּהָ בְּיָדֶךָ וְאֶל־בִּינָתְךָ אַל־תִּשָּׁעֵן:

יט רַבִּי יַנַּאי אוֹמֵר, אֵין בְּיָדֵינוּ לֹא מִשַּׁלְוַת הָרְשָׁעִים וְאַף לֹא מִיִּסּוּרֵי הַצַּדִּיקִים:

כ רַבִּי מַתְיָא בֶן־חָרָשׁ אוֹמֵר, הֱוֵי מַקְדִּים בִּשְׁלוֹם כָּל־אָדָם וֶהֱוֵי זָנָב לָאֲרָיוֹת וְאַל־תְּהִי רֹאשׁ לַשּׁוּעָלִים:

כא רַבִּי יַעֲקֹב אוֹמֵר, הָעוֹלָם הַזֶּה דּוֹמֶה לִפְרוֹזְדוֹר בִּפְנֵי הָעוֹלָם הַבָּא· הַתְקֵן עַצְמְךָ בַּפְּרוֹזְדוֹר כְּדֵי שֶׁתִּכָּנֵס לַטְּרַקְלִין:

כב הוּא הָיָה אוֹמֵר, יָפָה שָׁעָה אַחַת בִּתְשׁוּבָה וּמַעֲשִׂים טוֹבִים בָּעוֹלָם הַזֶּה מִכָּל חַיֵּי הָעוֹלָם הַבָּא וְיָפָה שָׁעָה אַחַת שֶׁל־קוֹרַת רוּחַ בָּעוֹלָם הַבָּא מִכָּל־חַיֵּי הָעוֹלָם הַזֶּה:

---

18. Seek out a place where the Torah is diligently studied, even if it means leaving your home that you love. Do not say that the wisdom of the Torah will be at your beck and call wherever you may be. For whatever skill you have will grow and survive only if you associate with people of similar interests. If you lack such companionship your talent—in this instance the knowledge of the Torah—will eventually atrophy.

19. To determine the relationship between the visible fate of a man and his moral worthiness or lack thereof is utterly beyond our power. It is not only the prosperity of the wicked that so frequently confronts us with an enigma. The fact that honest men should suffer seems just as perplexing, even though we believe that it is easier to assert that actually a person thus afflicted is wicked than to concede that he is good. The evil that a man does is never done under false pretenses, but the good he does may well be motivated by any number of considerations unknown to us, which are ignoble and thus cancel whatever value the supposed good deed might otherwise have had. However, we do not have sufficient insight either to determine a person's moral worth or worthlessness, or to judge whether that which befalls him is indeed a blessing or a calamity. Therefore it behooves us to abstain from passing judgment in either case, and not to permit our own short-sighted view of the events we witness to influence our own decisions.

18.   Rabbi Nehorai said: Emigrate to a place where there is Torah wisdom, and say not that it will follow you, for it is your associates who will keep it ever in your hand and do not rely upon your own understanding.

19.   Rabbi Yannai said: Nothing is in our hands; [we can explain] neither the prosperity of the lawless nor the sufferings of the righteous.

20.   Rabbi Mathyah ben Charash, said: Anticipate every man's salutation; be rather a tail among lions than a head among foxes.

21.   Rabbi Yaakov said: This world is like the vestibule before the world to come; prepare yourself in the vestibule so that you may [be able to] enter the banquet hall.

22.   He used to say: One hour of repentance and good deeds in this world is worth more than the whole life of the world to come; and one hour of spiritual bliss in the world to come is worth more than the whole life of this world.

---

20.   Do not expect others, as a sign of respect, to salute you first, but be the one to offer the first salute. Above all, seek the company of men who are superior to you both spiritually and morally, even though you would occupy an inferior position in their midst and would have to submit to their guidance. Conversely, shun any association with your moral and spiritual inferiors, even if you would stand out as a leader in their midst.

21.   All of us have been invited to the banquet of the King of Kings, but only he who has made himself worthy of this invitation will be admitted to the banquet hall. This world is the vestibule in which to prepare yourselves. Make use of your sojourn in the vestibule to make yourself worthy of entering the great hall itself.

22.   Each of these two worlds has its own purpose and thus a value peculiarly its own which the other cannot afford us. This world is the place where you may prepare yourself by self-ennoblement through the discharge of your physical, moral and spiritual tasks. You cannot make up in the world to come for any of the moral and spiritual refinement that you have not attained in this world by such faithful performance of your tasks. Hence even one hour of repentance and good deeds here on earth is more important for the improvement of your soul than all the life of the next; for that which you have failed to do in one hour of life's task here below you cannot retrieve even in all the eternity of the world to come. The world to come, on the other hand, is one of blissful happiness, and all the joys and pleasures which even the longest lifetime on earth could afford, cannot outweigh even one single hour of spiritual satisfaction such as is found in the world to come.

כג רַבִּי שִׁמְעוֹן בֶּן־אֶלְעָזָר אוֹמֵר, אַל־תְּרַצֶּה אֶת־חֲבֵרְךָ בִּשְׁעַת כַּעֲסוֹ וְאַל־תְּנַחֲמֶהוּ בְּשָׁעָה שֶׁמֵּתוֹ מֻטָּל לְפָנָיו · וְאַל־תִּשְׁאַל לוֹ בִּשְׁעַת נִדְרוֹ · וְאַל־תִּשְׁתַּדֵּל לִרְאוֹתוֹ בִּשְׁעַת קַלְקָלָתוֹ :

כד שְׁמוּאֵל הַקָּטָן אוֹמֵר, בִּנְפֹל אוֹיִבְךָ אַל־תִּשְׂמָח וּבִכָּשְׁלוֹ אַל־יָגֵל לִבֶּךָ · פֶּן־יִרְאֶה יְיָ וְרַע בְּעֵינָיו וְהֵשִׁיב מֵעָלָיו אַפּוֹ :

כה אֱלִישָׁע בֶּן־אֲבוּיָה אוֹמֵר, הַלּוֹמֵד יֶלֶד לְמָה הוּא דוֹמֶה לְדִיוֹ כְּתוּבָה עַל־נְיָר חָדָשׁ וְהַלּוֹמֵד זָקֵן לְמָה הוּא דוֹמֶה לִדְיוֹ כְּתוּבָה עַל־נְיָר מָחוּק :

כו רַבִּי יוֹסֵי בַּר יְהוּדָה אִישׁ כְּפַר הַבַּבְלִי אוֹמֵר, הַלּוֹמֵד מִן־הַקְּטַנִּים לְמָה הוּא דוֹמֶה לְאוֹכֵל עֲנָבִים קֵהוֹת וְשׁוֹתֶה יַיִן מִגִּתּוֹ וְהַלּוֹמֵד מִן־הַזְּקֵנִים לְמָה הוּא דוֹמֶה לְאוֹכֵל עֲנָבִים בְּשׁוּלוֹת וְשׁוֹתֶה יַיִן יָשָׁן :

כז רַבִּי (מֵאִיר) אוֹמֵר, אַל־תִּסְתַּכֵּל בַּקַּנְקַן אֶלָּא בְּמָה שֶׁיֶּשׁ־בּוֹ ·

---

23. When you seek to help your neighbor—wait for an appropriate time to do it. Do not think that good intentions alone are sufficient excuse and justification for all things. If you wish to influence your neighbor's mood, do not attempt to do so at the time when he is shaken and agitated, but wait until he has grown calmer and hence more amenable to reasonable suggestion. This rule holds true in whatever it is you seek to accomplish; whether it be to appease your fellow-man, or to comfort him, to spur him on to dissolve the vow he has made, or else to offer him your sympathy. — אל תשתדל Do not go out of your way to visit someone who suffered something unpleasant if you know that he would rather remain alone and unseen in his distress.

24. If your enemy who has pursued you should fall, do not rejoice, and if he commits a moral blunder do not exult in the knowledge that, at long last, the whole world will see how wicked he is. For if you were thus to gloat at another's misfortune, you would commit a grievous sin against God. It may very well be that God has tolerated your foe's pursuit of you only as a means to bring about your moral betterment. Your malicious joy at his downfall would then indicate to God that you have still not attained moral maturity;

23.   Rabbi Shimon ben Elazar, said: Seek not to appease your fellow-man at the time of his anger; nor to comfort him when his dead lies before him; nor suggest ways to reconsider his vow at the time he took it; and strive not to see him at the time of his humiliation.

24.   Shemuel Ha-Katan said: Rejoice not when your enemy falls, and let not your heart exult when he stumbles; lest the Lord see it and be displeased and He turn away his wrath from him.

25.   Elisha ben Abuyah, said: That which one learns in his youth is like ink written on clean paper; that which one learns in his old age is like ink written on blotted paper.

26.   Rabbi Yosé bar Yehudah, from Kfar Ha-Bavli, said: He who learns from young men is like one who eats unripe grapes and drinks wine from the wine press. He who learns from old men is like one who eats ripe grapes and drinks old wine.

27.   Rabbi Meir says: Look not at the vessel but at what it contains.

---

as a consequence, it may be that He will let your pursuer rise again in order to complete the process of your moral betterment. Shemuel Ha-Katan quotes this admonition from Prov. 24:17, 18 to remind himself and others, too, how closely we must guard at all times against entertaining any feeling of malice toward any of our fellow-men. It is not enough merely not to do evil to our foe and not to wish him ill. Even malicious joy at misfortune that came to him without any act on our part is a grievous sin indeed before the Lord.

25.   That which man learns in his youth he absorbs with an intellect still clear of other images and concepts; therefore that material which he then studies can leave a clear and lasting impression. But by the time a man is old, his mind is already prejudiced by much extraneous matter which must be pushed aside before the new can be accepted. Hence what he learns in his old age will not impress itself so easily upon his mind, nor deeply enough to remain with him permanently.

26.   While the most desirable students are young students, men of more mature age should be sought as teachers. Even as unripe grapes lack the ripeness acquired with time from the sun, so the knowledge which young men have absorbed and are able to communicate, lacks the mellowness that only years of experience and repeated reflection can afford. And even as wine newly taken from the press is still cloudy and unsettled, so the ideas which the young develop from the learning they have acquired and which they would pass on as truths based on solid knowledge still lack that calm and clear prudence by which the mature can sift the true from the false.

27.   Rabbi Meir points out, however, that the general statement set forth in Mishna 26 is not universally applicable. One should consider not so much

יֵשׁ קַנְקַן חָדָשׁ מָלֵא יָשָׁן·וְיָשָׁן שֶׁאֲפִלּוּ חָדָשׁ אֵין בּוֹ:

כח רַבִּי אֶלְעָזָר הַקַּפָּר אוֹמֵר, הַקִּנְאָה וְהַתַּאֲוָה וְהַכָּבוֹד מוֹצִיאִים אֶת־הָאָדָם מִן הָעוֹלָם:

כט הוּא הָיָה אוֹמֵר, הַיִּלּוֹדִים לָמוּת וְהַמֵּתִים לְהֵחָיוֹת וְהַחַיִּים לִדּוֹן, לֵידַע וּלְהוֹדִיעַ וּלְהִוָּדַע, שֶׁהוּא אֵל הוּא הַיּוֹצֵר הוּא הַבּוֹרֵא הוּא הַמֵּבִין הוּא הַדַּיָּן הוּא הָעֵד הוּא בַּעַל דִּין הוּא עָתִיד לָדוֹן בָּרוּךְ הוּא, שֶׁאֵין לְפָנָיו לֹא עַוְלָה וְלֹא שִׁכְחָה וְלֹא מַשּׂוֹא פָנִים וְלֹא מִקַּח שֹׁחַד, שֶׁהַכֹּל שֶׁלּוֹ·וְדַע שֶׁהַכֹּל לְפִי הַחֶשְׁבּוֹן וְאַל־יַבְטִיחֲךָ יִצְרֶךָ, שֶׁהַשְּׁאוֹל בֵּית מָנוֹס לָךְ, שֶׁעַל כָּרְחֲךָ אַתָּה נוֹצָר וְעַל כָּרְחֲךָ אַתָּה נוֹלָד וְעַל כָּרְחֲךָ אַתָּה חַי וְעַל כָּרְחֲךָ אַתָּה מֵת וְעַל כָּרְחֲךָ אַתָּה עָתִיד לִתֵּן דִּין וְחֶשְׁבּוֹן לִפְנֵי מֶלֶךְ מַלְכֵי הַמְּלָכִים הַקָּדוֹשׁ בָּרוּךְ הוּא:

רבי חנניא וכו׳ קדיש·

---

the age of the teacher as the content of the teaching that he has to offer. There are many young men whose minds are mature, while there are old men who do not possess even the knowledge of the young.

28. God caused man to live in the world and made him fit for it. It is only in connection with this world and through the endeavor to utilize his energies in the service of the world and its welfare that man fulfills his purpose. The vices listed here, however, make selfish interest the sole purpose of him whom they dominate and so they cause him to clash with the rest of the world, for under such circumstances the world has value to him only as long as it will cater to his desires. Thus he forfeits the destiny for which God made him.

29. Birth, death, resurrection and reckoning,—these are the preordained periods into which our lives are divided and of which we are to be aware at all times. We are to remember, always, that our life here below is bounded by death, but that death, too, is only a transient phase, leading to a new and different form of existence. Not only the soul is untouched by death but the body, too, is destined to live again. However with all of this we shall have to pass before the presence of the Lord in order to render accounting as to

There may be a new vessel full of old wine and an old vessel that has not even new wine in it.

28. Rabbi Elazar Ha-Kapar said: Envy, greed and thirst for honor take a man out from the world.

29. He used to say: Those who are born are destined to die, and the dead to rise again; the living, to be judged; to know, to teach and to make it known that God is the Maker, He the Creator, He the Discerner, He the Judge, He the Witness, He the Complainant. It is He that will in the future judge, blessed be He; in Whose presence there is no wrong, no forgetfulness, nor partiality, nor taking of bribes. Know also that everything comes to pass according to reckoning. And let not your fancy give you hope that the grave will be a place of refuge for you, for it was perforce that you were formed, perforce you were born, perforce you live, perforce you shall die, and perforce you will have to give account and reckoning before the Supreme King of Kings, the Holy One, blessed be He.

---

how and for what we have employed the life and existence granted us. — לידע ולהודיע ולהודע We ourselves are to know it, and to make others aware of it by teaching it to them, and, without explicit proclamation, we must let this truth become evident through everything we do, that God is not only the originator of our existence, but also that it was He Who shaped and fashioned us for our special purpose, and He carefully watches over our every step to discern whether or not we do justice to this our destiny. Therefore, if our behavior should not be in keeping with our Divinely-ordained destiny, God will also act as the Judge, Witness and Prosecutor and call us to account for our actions. In a court of justice over which a human judge presides, some human weakness on the part of the judge might save us, but in the Heavenly Tribunal there is no such chance. — הכל לפי החשבון The sentence does not depend upon the general impression left by the defendant; instead, it is determined by the accurate sum total of all our individual acts, both good and evil. Therefore let not even the smallest good that you accomplish, or even the least evil that you do, be a matter of indifference to you. For your every good deed adds to your merits before God, while every evil act of yours adds to the burden of your guilt. And there is no way for you to escape from this cycle that was preordained for you long before you were born; you have no choice with regard to either your creation or your birth, your life or your death, or with regard to your appearance before the Tribunal of God to render accounting for your past.

כל ישראל וכו'

א בַּעֲשָׂרָה מַאֲמָרוֹת נִבְרָא הָעוֹלָם· וּמַה תַּלְמוּד לוֹמַר וַהֲלֹא בְמַאֲמָר אֶחָד יָכוֹל לְהִבָּרְאוֹת, אֶלָּא לְהִפָּרַע מִן־הָרְשָׁעִים שֶׁמְּאַבְּדִים אֶת־הָעוֹלָם שֶׁנִּבְרָא בַּעֲשָׂרָה מַאֲמָרוֹת וְלִתֵּן שָׂכָר טוֹב לַצַּדִּיקִים שֶׁמְּקַיְּמִין אֶת־הָעוֹלָם שֶׁנִּבְרָא בַּעֲשָׂרָה מַאֲמָרוֹת:

ב עֲשָׂרָה דוֹרוֹת מֵאָדָם וְעַד נֹחַ לְהוֹדִיעַ כַּמָּה אֶרֶךְ אַפַּיִם לְפָנָיו שֶׁכָּל־הַדּוֹרוֹת הָיוּ מַכְעִיסִים לְפָנָיו עַד שֶׁהֵבִיא עֲלֵיהֶם אֶת־מֵי הַמַּבּוּל:

ג עֲשָׂרָה דוֹרוֹת מִנֹּחַ וְעַד אַבְרָהָם, לְהוֹדִיעַ כַּמָּה אֶרֶךְ אַפַּיִם לְפָנָיו, שֶׁכָּל־הַדּוֹרוֹת הָיוּ מַכְעִיסִים לְפָנָיו עַד שֶׁבָּא אַבְרָהָם אָבִינוּ וְקִבֵּל (עָלָיו) שְׂכַר כֻּלָּם:

ד עֲשָׂרָה נִסְיוֹנוֹת נִתְנַסָּה אַבְרָהָם אָבִינוּ וְעָמַד בְּכֻלָּם לְהוֹדִיעַ כַּמָּה חִבָּתוֹ שֶׁל־אַבְרָהָם אָבִינוּ:

---

1. Had the entire process of Creation been completed by one single Divine utterance, and had it been thus recorded for us in the Torah also, then all things, the whole and all the parts thereof, would have appeared to be im-mediately caused by God's command of Creation only, and the position of man in the scheme of things would have been fixed on one plane with that of all the other works of creation. However, in this world, which was led to greater perfection by ten different utterances of Creation, one following the other, all the things that were made first were contributing factors in the creation of what came after them, and were, in fact, completed by the latter. Hence all that which came into being at a later time represents the completion of what has gone before and, in fact, is dependent upon the latter. All things sustain and are sustained in their turn. Man is the final work of creation, the goal and summit of the whole, in whom all of creation culminates. But his existence and his efficacy, too, are dependent upon the existence and the efficacy of all the rest of the world. If man fulfills his great task, then all the world of creation will attain through him the prerequisite for its survival. Hence, with the care that man extends to even the most minute fraction of the world entity in line with his task and duty, he makes a contribution not only

1.   By ten utterances was the world created. What does this teach us? Could it not [all] have been created by one utterance? It is only to call to account the lawless who destroy the world that was created by ten utterances, and to give good reward to the righteous who preserve the world that was created by ten utterances.

2.   There were ten generations from Adam to Noach, to show how long-suffering He is, seeing that all these generations acted contrary to His will, until He brought upon them the waters of lifelessness.

3.   There were ten generations from Noach to Avraham, to show how long-suffering He is, seeing that all these generations acted contrary to His will, until our Father Avraham came and earned for himself the merit of them all.

4.   With ten trials was our Father Avraham tried and he stood firm through them all, to show how great was the love of our Father Avraham for God.

---

to his own survival but also to that of the whole. But if man, in criminal lawlessness, should cast away his great destiny, he will only help prejudice the survival of the whole of creation, and by his unlawful destruction or neglect of even one fraction of the whole, he destroys and neglects that upon which depends not only his own salvation, but that of all the rest of creation as well.

2.   היו מכעיסים: They stirred up, or evoked, His wrath; they were fully deserving of His anger. But God, being slow to anger, allowed them time to repent until the days of Noah.

3.   קבל שכר כולם Every single member of the generations preceding Abraham should have felt himself called upon to counteract the steadily spreading evil and to pave the way for a better future. But it was only Abraham who earned the merit and was found worthy of being chosen as the instrument for bringing about that better future.

4.   חבתו של אברהם אבינו. According to the context, it would seem that חבתו של אברהם אבינו has an active connotation, denoting Abraham's love for God. If, however, one should wish to construe this phrase in the more customary manner, that is, as denoting the love of God for Abraham, then the repeated trials should be taken as evidence in themselves of the high regard in which God held Abraham. As the Mishna has it: "The potter will strike only those pots that are good and whole to test them, because he knows that they will withstand even repeated blows."

ה. עֲשָׂרָה נִסִּים נַעֲשׂוּ לַאֲבוֹתֵינוּ בְּמִצְרַיִם וַעֲשָׂרָה עַל הַיָּם:

י. עֶשֶׂר מַכּוֹת הֵבִיא הַקָּדוֹשׁ בָּרוּךְ הוּא עַל הַמִּצְרִיִּים בְּמִצְרַיִם וְעֶשֶׂר עַל הַיָּם:

ז. עֲשָׂרָה נִסְיוֹנוֹת נִסּוּ אֲבוֹתֵינוּ אֶת־הַקָּדוֹשׁ בָּרוּךְ הוּא בַּמִּדְבָּר שֶׁנֶּאֱמַר וַיְנַסּוּ אֹתִי זֶה עֶשֶׂר פְּעָמִים וְלֹא שָׁמְעוּ בְּקוֹלִי:

ח. עֲשָׂרָה נִסִּים נַעֲשׂוּ לַאֲבוֹתֵינוּ בְּבֵית הַמִּקְדָּשׁ · לֹא הִפִּילָה אִשָּׁה מֵרֵיחַ בְּשַׂר הַקֹּדֶשׁ, וְלֹא הִסְרִיחַ בְּשַׂר הַקֹּדֶשׁ מֵעוֹלָם, וְלֹא נִרְאָה זְבוּב בְּבֵית הַמִּטְבָּחַיִם, וְלֹא אֵרַע קֶרִי לְכֹהֵן גָּדוֹל בְּיוֹם הַכִּפּוּרִים, וְלֹא כִבּוּ הַגְּשָׁמִים אֵשׁ שֶׁל־עֲצֵי הַמַּעֲרָכָה, וְלֹא נִצְּחָה הָרוּחַ אֶת־עַמּוּד הֶעָשָׁן, וְלֹא נִמְצָא פְסוּל בָּעֹמֶר וּבִשְׁתֵּי הַלֶּחֶם וּבְלֶחֶם הַפָּנִים, עוֹמְדִים צְפוּפִים וּמִשְׁתַּחֲוִים רְוָחִים וְלֹא הִזִּיק נָחָשׁ וְעַקְרָב בִּירוּשָׁלַיִם מֵעוֹלָם, וְלֹא אָמַר אָדָם לַחֲבֵרוֹ צַר לִי הַמָּקוֹם שֶׁאָלִין בִּירוּשָׁלָיִם:

ט. עֲשָׂרָה דְבָרִים נִבְרְאוּ בְּעֶרֶב שַׁבָּת בֵּין הַשְּׁמָשׁוֹת וְאֵלּוּ הֵן·

6. We have but scant knowledge of these עֶשֶׂר מַכּוֹת which struck the Egyptians at the Reed Sea. The miracles which our fathers experienced both in Mitzrayim and at the Reed Sea consisted primarily in the fact that they remained untouched by the plagues with which the Egyptians were stricken.

7. These repeated incidents of doubt and mutiny against the Will of God which marked the wanderings of our fathers in the wilderness are certainly ample proof for him who desires it that, contrary to what many would like to have themselves and others believe, the Torah did not originate with the Jewish people. Unlike all other codes of religious law, the Jewish "religion" and the Jewish law did *not* originate and emanate from *within* the people but were handed to it from *without,* thus of metaphysical origin, and proceeded to establish its Divine power in the ultimate conquest of the people. This people was to undergo an unparalleled martyrdom of many centuries for the very law against which it had resisted so stubbornly in the beginning. Similarly, the repeated instances of doubt are, in fact, a truly valid guarantee

5. Ten miracles were wrought for our fathers in *Mitzrayim* and ten at the Sea.

6. Ten plagues did the Holy One, blessed be He, bring upon the Egyptians in Egypt and ten at the Sea.

7. Ten times did our fathers try the Holy One, blessed be He, in the wilderness, as it is said, "Now they have tried me ten times and have not listened to My voice."

8. Ten miracles were wrought for our fathers in the Temple Sanctuary: No woman miscarried from the scent of the sacrificial meat; the sacrificial meat never became putrid; no fly was ever seen in the slaughter house of the Temple; no unclean accident ever befell the High Priest on the Day of Atonement; the rain never extinguished the fire on the wood pile on the altar; the wind did not prevail over the column of smoke that rose from the altar; no disqualifying defect was ever found in the Omer, in the two Shevuoth loaves or in the show-breads. [The people] stood closely pressed together and yet found ample space to prostrate themselves; no snake or scorpion ever did injury in Jerusalem, and no man ever said to his fellow: "There is too little room for me to lodge overnight in Jerusalem."

9. Ten things were created on the [first] Sabbath Eve at twilight:

---

for the factual truth of the Divine Revelation and the Divine miracles which accompanied the creation of our people and which we proclaimed to mankind. They demonstrate that the generation which partook of this Divine revelation and guidance was not composed of naive and credulous men who were ready to subscribe unconditionally to these new and unprecedented phenomena and events. This was—as they are described by our Sages—a דור דעה, a "sophisticated" generation which recognized and acknowledged the revealed demonstrations of Divinity only after repeated trials. Thus, in the end, it was not on the basis of "convenient belief" but with the "conviction of knowledge" based on the truth that they were ready to fight for and defend that which they had recognized to be the essence of their very existence.

8. These miraculous occurrences bore testimony to the constant presence of God both in the Holy City and in the Sanctuary, safeguarding the sacred rites performed in these holy places.

9. The creative process that took place during the Six Days of Creation embraces all the visible world. The Seventh Day, the Sabbath, is the memorial to the unseen Creator and Master of the world; it serves to train man to recognize and render homage to this his unseen Lord and Maker. In keeping

פִּי הָאָרֶץ פִּי הַבְּאֵר פִּי הָאָתוֹן הַקֶּשֶׁת וְהַמָּן וְהַמַּטֶּה וְהַשָּׁמִיר
הַכְּתָב וְהַמִּכְתָב וְהַלֻחוֹת · וְיֵשׁ אוֹמְרִים אַף הַמַּזִּיקִין וּקְבוּרָתוֹ
שֶׁל־מֹשֶׁה וְאֵילוֹ שֶׁל־אַבְרָהָם אָבִינוּ וְיֵשׁ אוֹמְרִים אַף צְבַת
בִּצְבַת עֲשׂוּיָה :

׳ שִׁבְעָה דְבָרִים בַּגֹּלֶם וְשִׁבְעָה בֶּחָכָם· חָכָם אֵינוֹ מְדַבֵּר
לִפְנֵי מִי שֶׁגָּדוֹל מִמֶּנוּ בַּחָכְמָה וּבְמִנְיָן, וְאֵינוֹ נִכְנָס לְתוֹךְ דִּבְרֵי
חֲבֵרוֹ, וְאֵינוֹ נִבְהָל לְהָשִׁיב, שׁוֹאֵל כָּעִנְיָן וּמֵשִׁיב כַּהֲלָכָה,

---

with their nature, the things enumerated here are part of the physical world which was made during the first days of Creation. But their purpose is more in keeping with that of the Seventh Day, because, like the Sabbath, they, too, have the function of training man for his moral destiny. Thus they stand midway, as it were, between the works of the Six Days, and the Sabbath, forming a transition from the one to the other. — פי הארץ refers to the gaping hole that opened up to swallow Korah and his kin to demonstrate that Moses had indeed been sent by God and that therefore any mutiny against him or denial of his mission was a criminal act. — פי הבאר denotes the Well of Miriam which accompanied our fathers in the wilderness and thus made their every drink of water a testimony to the presence of Divine Providence. — פי האתון alludes to the faculty of speech that was temporarily given the she-ass to humble Bileam, to teach a lesson to that man of brilliant speech at the moment when, led by base passion and impudent conceit, he sought to misuse his human gift of speech to curse a whole nation. — קשת refers to the rainbow which God caused to appear after the Flood as an eternal symbol of His patience with human error. — מן is the heavenly Mannah which, like no other act of Divine sovereignty, bore testimony to the care with which God remembers every living thing, and which was to teach men to trust in God and cheerfully to obey Him not only then, but throughout all the generations to come. — המטה is the staff of Moses which served as the visible symbol of God's intervention in His own world order to train man and to chastise him for his disobedience and his pusillanimity. — שמיר was the worm which was employed in the erection of the Sanctuary to cut stones when the use of ordinary metal cutting or cleaving tools was forbidden. — הכתב: In the case of the first Tablets of the Law not only the writing as such, but the Tablets as well were the work of God Himself, as it is written והלוחות מעשה אלקים המה and והמכתב מכתב אלקים (Exod. 32:16). But as for the second set of Ten Commandments, though once again God Himself had written the words, it was Moses who had hewed out the stone tablets as it is written פסל לך שני לחות

the Mouth of the Earth, the Mouth of the Well, the Mouth of the She-ass, the Rainbow, the Mannah, the Staff, the Shamir, the Written Characters, the Writing, and the Tablets. Some say: the *Mazikin* also, and the grave of Moshe, and the ram of our Father Avraham. Others say: Also the tongs made by means of tongs.

10. There are seven marks of a boor and seven of a wise man. The wise man does not speak before him who is greater than he is in wisdom and experience; he does not interrupt the speech of his companion. He is not hasty to answer; he asks questions in keeping with the subject and answers to the point. He speaks of the first thing first

---

אבנים ... וכתבתי על הלחות את הדברים וגו' (Exod. 34:1). In view of the foregoing, the word הכתב would refer to the second set of Tablets, while והמכתב would allude to the first. — מזיקין : It is difficult to determine with any degree of certainty what is meant by this term. At any rate, as the term itself implies and as is indicated in Berachoth 6a, it alludes to those influences which are detrimental or "damaging" to continued human welfare. According to this view, the Mazikin, too, belonged to those factors which, while in themselves part of the physical world, served the advancement of man's moral and spiritual salvation.—Because no one knows where it may be found, (Deut. 34:6) the grave of Moses, too, helps advance our spiritual and moral salvation. For were its site known, ceaseless pilgrimages would have given rise to a cult of quasi-idolatry which would have been most detrimental to our spiritual welfare. — אילו של א"א :This is the ram which presented itself to Abraham for sacrifice after God had told him to spare Isaac, his son. Thus the ram became the symbol of all future sacrifices by which man selflessly pledges all of his being, his skills, his endeavors and his achievement to the fulfillment of God's will for all the times to come. — צבת : This statement is based on the premise that even the original pair of tongs was made with a special pair of tongs produced by Divine providence to handle the red-hot metal out of which this, the first tool, was then formed. In other words, even as it was God Himself Who gave man his first garment (Gen. 3:21), so, too, man received his first tool directly from the hands of God, thus implying that industry, like clothing, should also be dedicated to fulfill a higher moral purpose.

10. אינו מדבר לפני וכו' : He does not speak before the others do, and he allows those who are wiser and more experienced than he to voice their opinions first. ובמנין : i.e. greater experience either in terms of the number of years lived or in terms of the number of disciples taught. Both of these factors make for experience, and we have made our translation convey this thought. ואומר על ראשון:His speech is logical; he mentions and discusses the subjects in their logical sequence. מודה על האמת:He does not stubbornly insist upon the validity of a statement which he has made once. If he sees, or learns, that he has

וְאוֹמֵר עַל־רִאשׁוֹן רִאשׁוֹן וְעַל־אַחֲרוֹן, וְעַל מַה־שֶּׁלֹּא
שָׁמַע אוֹמֵר לֹא שָׁמָעְתִּי, וּמוֹדֶה עַל־הָאֱמֶת, וְחִלּוּפֵיהֶן בְּגֹלֶם:

יא שִׁבְעָה מִינֵי פוּרְעָנִיּוֹת בָּאִין לָעוֹלָם עַל־שִׁבְעָה גוּפֵי עֲבֵרָה:
מִקְצָתָן מְעַשְּׂרִין וּמִקְצָתָן אֵינָן מְעַשְּׂרִין רָעָב שֶׁל־בַּצֹּרֶת
בָּא מִקְצָתָן רְעֵבִים וּמִקְצָתָן שְׂבֵעִים: נָמְרוּ שֶׁלֹּא לְעַשֵּׂר רָעָב
שֶׁל מְהוּמָה וְשֶׁל־בַּצֹּרֶת בָּא: וְשֶׁלֹּא לִטּוֹל אֶת־הַחַלָּה רָעָב
שֶׁל־כְּלָיָה בָּא: הֶבֶר בָּא לָעוֹלָם עַל־מִיתוֹת הָאֲמוּרוֹת בַּתּוֹרָה
שֶׁלֹּא נִמְסְרוּ לְבֵית דִּין וְעַל פֵּרוֹת שְׁבִיעִית: חֶרֶב בָּאָה לָעוֹלָם

made an error, he will be ready and willing to concede that he has been wrong.

11. The laws pertaining to מעשר; that is, the מעשר ראשון, "the Levite's tithe"; מעשר שני, the tithe to be eaten in the Holy City; and מעשר עני, the tithe to be set aside for the poor, symbolize claims made upon the blessed harvest for things of the spirit, for the hallowing of physical enjoyment and for the practical demonstration of altruism. The law concerning the חלה, the separation of the bread dough, teaches every individual to view his own share in the general harvest as a special demonstration of God's care and providence, and to consider the devoted study and fulfillment of the Law of God an obligation incumbent upon each and every man to discharge in return for that Divine care. If these laws which pertain to the fruits of the soil are neglected or ignored in any manner, then the spiritual elements of life, its moral consecration, the love of man and the fear of God that should be part of the life which the harvest was meant to preserve, will give way to desecration, profanation, selfishness and godlessness And to the extent that godlessness is on the rise, God will cause the blessings of the harvest to decrease and finally to be absent altogether.

מיתות וגו׳ שלא נמסרו לב״ד: The capital transgression which the criminal cannot expiate by way of the intervention of an earthly court of justice. פרות שביעית All those fruits that grow untended during the Sabbatical year are to be consecrated as a tribute to God, the original Owner and Master of the soil. Therefore our right to make use of them is circumscribed by law and any transgression of those limitations would constitute an act of contempt and mutiny against the sovereignty of God. He who is guilty of a capital transgression and has not expiated for it thus forfeits the right to existence, and he who mutinies against the sovereignty of God thereby forfeits the right to remain on the earth which is the Lord's. In such cases it is a fate of death decreed by God that acts as the executioner.

and of the last last. Regarding that which he has not learned, he says,
"I have not learned this" and he acknowledges the truth. The reverse
of all this is to be found in the boor.

11.   Seven kinds of punishment come into the world for seven kinds
of transgressions: If some give their tithes and others do not, there
will be famine from dearth and some will suffer hunger while others
will have plenty. If they have all ceased to give tithes there will be
a famine caused by panic and dearth. If they have all ceased to take
Hallah from their dough there will be a famine of extermination.
Pestilence comes into the world to execute those death penalties enumerated in the Torah which are not within the purview of the Court
of Justice, and for the violations involving the fruits of the Seventh
Year. The sword comes into the world for the delay of justice, for

---

חרב : The Lord conferred statehood upon His people so that they might
defend the enforcement of justice and preserve the truth contained in our
Law as handed down by transmission. If the Jewish State will carry out this
mission, it can be sure of Divine support against all enemy powers, and no
other nation will dare attack it. But if the Jewish State should cast off its
task and destiny or put it to wrongful use, it will thereby become a nation
at the mercy of fate just like all the other states of the world, and God will
withdraw His protection from it. As a human power, the Jewish State has
always been at a disadvantage when set off against the other nations; therefore, once Divine protection is denied the Jewish State, hostile powers will
not hesitate to wield the sword against it.

חיה רעה : As long as man will submit to God and remain erect by virtue
of his obedience, the beast will retreat before him in awe. But if, by indifference to the sacred nature of a vow, he will deny his allegiance to God or
actually contravene it, so that as a result of his conduct the homage of others
to God will be lessened, too, the beast will no longer view him as its superior,
as the master before whom it must timidly keep its distance, and will attack
him גלות : עבודה זרה, גלוי עריות and שפיכות דמים are the capital transgressions
against the fundamentals of that Law for the sake of which God had originally
promised and given us the Holy Land. These deadly sins constitute violations
of the reverence due God, of the respect due oneself and of the regard we
owe to our neighbors. שמטה. The law commanding us to let our land lie
fallow during the Sabbatical year is the great public proclamation that God
is the Ruler and Owner of the land which He turned over to us with the
explicit stipulation that we acknowledge His sovereignty and carry out his
will as laid down in His Law. Hence, if the inhabitants of God's land so
far forget their God and their duty to Him that they commit any of the

עַל־עִנּוּי הַדִּין וְעַל־עִוּוּת הַדִּין וְעַל־הַמּוֹרִים בַּתּוֹרָה, שֶׁלֹּא
כַהֲלָכָה: חַיָּה רָעָה בָּאָה לָעוֹלָם עַל־שְׁבוּעַת שָׁוְא וְעַל־חִלּוּל
הַשֵּׁם: גָּלוּת בָּאָה לָעוֹלָם עַל־עוֹבְדֵי אֱלִילִים וְעַל־גִּלּוּי עֲרָיוֹת
וְעַל־שְׁפִיכוּת דָּמִים וְעַל־שְׁמִטַּת הָאָרֶץ:

יב בְּאַרְבָּעָה פְרָקִים הַדֶּבֶר מִתְרַבֶּה, בָּרְבִיעִית וּבַשְּׁבִיעִית
וּבְמוֹצָאֵי שְׁבִיעִית וּבְמוֹצָאֵי הֶחָג שֶׁבְּכָל־שָׁנָה וְשָׁנָה: בָּרְבִיעִית
מִפְּנֵי מַעְשַׂר עָנִי שֶׁבַּשְּׁלִישִׁית בַּשְּׁבִיעִית מִפְּנֵי מַעְשַׂר עָנִי
שֶׁבַּשִּׁשִּׁית, בְּמוֹצָאֵי שְׁבִיעִית מִפְּנֵי פֵרוֹת שְׁבִיעִית, בְּמוֹצָאֵי הֶחָג
שֶׁבְּכָל־שָׁנָה וְשָׁנָה מִפְּנֵי גֶזֶל מַתְּנוֹת עֲנִיִּים:

יג אַרְבַּע מִדּוֹת בָּאָדָם · הָאוֹמֵר שֶׁלִּי שֶׁלִּי וְשֶׁלְּךָ שֶׁלָּךְ זוֹ
מִדָּה בֵינוֹנִית וְיֵשׁ אוֹמְרִים זוֹ מִדַּת סְדוֹם, שֶׁלִּי שֶׁלָּךְ וְשֶׁלְּךָ
שֶׁלִּי עַם הָאָרֶץ, שֶׁלִּי (שֶׁלָּךְ) וְשֶׁלְּךָ שֶׁלָּךְ חָסִיד, שֶׁלִּי (שֶׁלָּךְ)
וְשֶׁלְּךָ שֶׁלִּי רָשָׁע:

---

first three transgressions named here, or else that they publicly deny His
supreme sovereignty by violating the *Shemittah* law, these criminal acts in
themselves will serve to condemn them to expulsion and banishment from
their homeland.

12. If, even in times of general calamity such as pestilence, the people should
deprive the poor of the gifts lawfully due them, this alone would be sufficient
reason for a worsening of the epidemic. During the third and sixth of the
seven-year *Shemittah* cycle the second tithe, which during other years had to
be eaten in Jerusalem, would be turned over to the poor. Those fruits and
vegetables that grew untended during the Sabbatical year were regarded as
ownerless and the poor were permitted to benefit from them.—The מתנות עניים
are the gifts set aside for the poor from the harvest each year, such as לקט,
שכחה, פאה, etc.

13. It would seem that the view that every person should keep that which
is his and that no one else should derive benefit from the property of another
is midway between good and evil. Some, however, feel that it is a most reprehensible attitude because it would expunge from the human heart and mind
that guiding principle of loving-kindness without which man would lose his

the perversion of justice and on those who do not teach the Law in accordance with the transmitted interpretation. Wild beasts come into the world because of perjury and the profanation of the Divine Name. Exile comes into the world because of idolatry, immorality, murder, and the non-observance of the year of rest for the soil.

12. At four periods does pestilence increase: in the fourth year, in the seventh, and at the conclusion of the seventh year, and at the conclusion of the Feast of Tabernacles in every year. In the fourth year for failure to give the tithe to the poor in the third year; in the seventh year for failure to give the tithe to the poor in the sixth year; at the conclusion of the seventh year for transgressions involving the fruits of the Seventh Year; at the conclusion of the Feast of Tabernacles in every year for depriving the poor of the gifts lawfully due them.

13. There are four character types among men: He who says: "What is mine is mine, and what is yours is yours" is an average character; some say that this is the character of Sodom. He who says: "What is mine is yours and what is yours is mine" is an ignoramus. [He who says] "What is mine is yours and what is yours is yours" is godly; [He who says] "What is yours is mine and what is mine is mine," is a lawless man.

Divinely-given nobility, and human society would be deprived of the goal ordained for it as its destiny. The second alternative, שלי שלך ושלך שלי, to abolish all private ownership and institute the common holding of property, is likewise based on deplorable ignorance. For its practical implementation would not only cancel the sanctity of the individual's right to own property and thus his one possibility for true independence, but it would also deprive man of the opportunity to practice mercy of his own free will. For I practice mercy, only if, of my own free will and sense of duty, I give to another that which it would be my right to keep for myself and which he has no legal right to demand from me. If I were to give to my fellow-man only that which he would be entitled to take by himself even without my consent, there will certainly be no love between us. It is only where justice is recognized that there is room also for loving-kindness, and conversely it is only where mercy, too, is a motivating power that justice can attain its goal which is to advance the general welfare. Justice is the foundation of society, and mercy is its finishing touch. He who has the virtue of חסידות, who shows practical piety by acts of loving-kindness will say: "I shall give to all others of that which is mine, and I will make no claims upon them in return: שלי שלך and שלך שלך."

יד אַרְבַּע מִדּוֹת בְּדֵעוֹת · נוֹחַ לִכְעוֹס וְנוֹחַ לִרְצוֹת יָצָא הֶפְסֵדוֹ בִּשְׂכָרוֹ, קָשֶׁה לִכְעוֹס וְקָשֶׁה לִרְצוֹת יָצָא שְׂכָרוֹ בְּהֶפְסֵדוֹ, קָשֶׁה לִכְעוֹס וְנוֹחַ לִרְצוֹת חָסִיד, נוֹחַ לִכְעוֹס וְקָשֶׁה לִרְצוֹת רָשָׁע:

טו אַרְבַּע מִדּוֹת בְּתַלְמִידִים · מָהִיר לִשְׁמוֹעַ וּמָהִיר לְאַבֵּד יָצָא שְׂכָרוֹ בְּהֶפְסֵדוֹ, קָשֶׁה לִשְׁמוֹעַ וְקָשֶׁה לְאַבֵּד יָצָא הֶפְסֵדוֹ בִּשְׂכָרוֹ, מָהִיר לִשְׁמוֹעַ וְקָשֶׁה לְאַבֵּד זוֹ חֵלֶק טוֹב, קָשֶׁה לִשְׁמוֹעַ וּמָהִיר לְאַבֵּד זוֹ חֵלֶק רָע:

טז אַרְבַּע מִדּוֹת בְּנוֹתְנֵי צְדָקָה · הָרוֹצֶה שֶׁיִּתֵּן וְלֹא יִתְּנוּ אֲחֵרִים עֵינוֹ רָעָה בְּשֶׁל־אֲחֵרִים, יִתְּנוּ אֲחֵרִים וְהוּא לֹא יִתֵּן עֵינוֹ רָעָה בְּשֶׁלּוֹ, יִתֵּן וְיִתְּנוּ אֲחֵרִים חָסִיד, לֹא יִתֵּן וְלֹא יִתְּנוּ אֲחֵרִים רָשָׁע:

---

14. נוח לרצות The person who is ready not only להתרצות "to let himself be pacified" but who, once he was angry or has been provoked to wrath, will calm down by himself (לרצות) without the persuasion of others, is blessed with a good disposition. It is so deeply rooted in basic goodness of the heart that it will outweigh even the weakness of נוח לכעוס of being easy to anger, for which, of course, we hold no brief. Even if he should become angry, a person of such disposition will quickly repent of his wrath and will show that he regrets his conduct. He will be kindly disposed toward all his fellow-men and his innate kindness will enable him to maintain at all times that type of disposition which will make him a joy both to himself and to those about him. Not so the person who, though slow to anger, is most difficult to appease once he has been provoked and nurses his resentment, bearing a smoldering grudge in his heart long after the untoward incident has passed. That type of person, as a rule, holds too high an estimate of himself and of what others owe to him. His heart lacks that goodness which makes man noble and more like His God Who is נושא עון ועובר על פשע. And since in this world there is no lack of just cause for wrath, the weakness of being קשה לרצות will readily give rise to a disposition that can make a man remain permanently at odds with those about him; hence יצא שכרו בהפסדו.

15. Frequently quick forgetting is a result of too great speed and ease in learning. Because the student of that type need not exert himself to under-

14. There are four kinds of disposition: He who is easy to provoke and easy to pacify—his loss disappears in his gain. He who is hard to provoke and hard to pacify—his gain disappears in his loss. He who is hard to provoke and easy to pacify is a godly man. He who is easy to provoke and hard to pacify is a lawless man.

15. There are four types of students: Quick to learn and quick to forget—his gain disappears in his loss. Slow to learn and slow to forget—his loss disappears in his gain. Quick to learn and slow to forget is the best portion. Slow to learn and quick to forget is the worst portion.

16. There are four types of donors to charity. He who desires to give but not that others should give, begrudges the privilege of others. He who desires that others should give but will not give himself is grudging of his own. He who desires that both he and others should give is pious. He who will not give and does not want others to give is lawless.

---

stand the lecture material, he will learn it only superficially, and he will make no great effort to retain it, for he will say to himself that, if he should forget it, he will have no trouble re-learning it whenever he should so desire. A student who has more difficulty in learning has an advantage over him, for by virtue of the effort and repeated study in which he must engage in order to learn, he has better impressed the material upon his memory. Thus, while in the first instance, the weakness of forgetfulness cancels out the talent of ease in learning, so the virtue of better retention here cancels out the handicap of difficulty in learning.

16. It is somewhat difficult to determine the manner in which to construe בשלו and עינו רעה בשל אחרים and הרוצה וכו' ולא יתנו אחרים. It appears that these statements are severe criticisms of the view according to which it is a meritorious deed to refrain from persuading others to give charity or even actually to prevent them from doing so, in the erroneous opinion that one does them a service by thus helping them keep their fortune intact. People with an erroneous attitude such as this neither know nor understand that, in fact, it is primarily that wealth which is spent on good works that truly becomes the permanent possession of its giver, benefitting him by advancing his eternal salvation. Thus to restrain oneself or others from giving charity is not an act of kindness at all, but actually a disservice both to oneself and one's fellows.

יז אַרְבַּע מִדּוֹת בְּהוֹלְכֵי בֵית הַמִּדְרָשׁ · הוֹלֵךְ וְאֵינוֹ עֹשֶׂה שְׂכַר הֲלִיכָה בְּיָדוֹ, עֹשֶׂה וְאֵינוֹ הוֹלֵךְ שְׂכַר מַעֲשֶׂה בְּיָדוֹ, הוֹלֵךְ וְעֹשֶׂה, חָסִיד, לֹא הוֹלֵךְ וְלֹא עֹשֶׂה רָשָׁע:

יח אַרְבַּע מִדּוֹת בְּיוֹשְׁבִים לִפְנֵי חֲכָמִים, סְפוֹג וּמַשְׁפֵּךְ מְשַׁמֶּרֶת וְנָפָה · סְפוֹג שֶׁהוּא סוֹפֵג אֶת־הַכֹּל, וּמַשְׁפֵּךְ שֶׁמַּכְנִיס בְּזוֹ וּמוֹצִיא בְזוֹ, מְשַׁמֶּרֶת שֶׁמּוֹצִיאָה אֶת־הַיַּיִן וְקוֹלֶטֶת אֶת־הַשְּׁמָרִים, וְנָפָה שֶׁמּוֹצִיאָה אֶת־הַקֶּמַח וְקוֹלֶטֶת אֶת־הַסֹּלֶת:

יט כָּל־אַהֲבָה שֶׁהִיא־תְלוּיָה בְדָבָר בָּטֵל דָּבָר בְּטֵלָה אַהֲבָה, וְשֶׁאֵינָהּ תְּלוּיָה בְדָבָר אֵינָהּ בְּטֵלָה לְעוֹלָם · אֵיזוֹ הִיא אַהֲבָה שֶׁהִיא־תְלוּיָה בְדָבָר זוֹ אַהֲבַת אַמְנוֹן וְתָמָר, וְשֶׁאֵינָהּ תְּלוּיָה בְדָבָר זוֹ אַהֲבַת דָּוִד וִיהוֹנָתָן:

---

17. In the days of the Mishna one had to attend lectures at the house of study if one desired to "learn" because the Oral Teaching had not yet been put down in writing. Thus attendance at the house of study was synonymous with what we know today as "learning". By virtue of the fact that the Tradition was thus taught by direct communication through the living world and studied in communion with many others, such "learning" in the house of study was, in fact, made all the more fruitful. We are told in this Mishna that even he who, though regularly attending the house of study, does not put into practice what he has learned there has reaped at least some benefit from his attendance at the classes. It is inevitable that his mind and spirit should absorb at least a part of what he has heard there, and we know that repeated study eventually leads to observance in practice. Conversely, even he who does not neglect to keep the Law in practice, but on the other hand does not make the effort continuously to amend, enrich and perfect his knowledge of the

17. There are four types among those who attend the house of study. He who attends the house of study but does not practice [its teachings] still secures the reward for attending. He who practices [its teachings] but does not attend the house of study secures the reward for practicing. He who attends [there] and practices is godly; he who neither attends nor practices is lawless.

18. There are four types of those who sit before the Sages; a sponge, a funnel, a strainer and a sieve. A sponge which absorbs everything; a funnel, which lets in at one end and out at the other; a strainer which lets the wine pass out and retains the sediment; and a sieve which lets out the bran-dust and retains the fine flour.

19. All such love as depends on a [physical] cause will pass away once the cause is no longer there, but that love which is not dependent on a [physical] cause will never pass away. Which love was dependent on a [physical] cause? The love of Amnon and Tamar. And which love depended on no such cause? The love of David and Yonathan.

Law's requirements through regular "learning" at the house of study will not fail to reap some profit through his law-abiding conduct. Yet his gain would be infinitely greater and constantly growing if, in addition, he were to increase his knowledge and ennoble his character by means of faithful, regular study.

18. נפה   As we learn from Menachoth 76b, the grains of wheat, after separation from the chaff, were repeatedly shaken in a sieve to eliminate the קמח, the inferior flour dust which forms the outer layer. Then only the סולת, the fine inner kernel would be retained in the sieve. This should explain the simile employed in the above Mishna.

19. Wherever love is rooted in the spiritual and moral worth of the beloved person, there the love will be as abiding as the values on which it is founded. But a love based on physical attraction will not outlast those fleeting charms.

כ כָּל־מַחֲלֹקֶת שֶׁהִיא לְשֵׁם שָׁמַיִם סוֹפָהּ לְהִתְקַיֵּם וְשֶׁאֵינָהּ לְשֵׁם שָׁמַיִם אֵין סוֹפָהּ לְהִתְקַיֵּם · אֵיזוֹ הִיא מַחֲלֹקֶת שֶׁהִיא לְשֵׁם שָׁמַיִם זוֹ מַחֲלֹקֶת הִלֵּל וְשַׁמַּאי, וְשֶׁאֵינָהּ לְשֵׁם שָׁמַיִם זוֹ מַחֲלֹקֶת קֹרַח וְכָל־עֲדָתוֹ :

כא כָּל־הַמְזַכֶּה אֶת־הָרַבִּים אֵין חֵטְא בָּא עַל־יָדוֹ וְכָל־הַמַּחֲטִיא אֶת־הָרַבִּים אֵין־מַסְפִּיקִין בְּיָדוֹ לַעֲשׂוֹת תְּשׁוּבָה · מֹשֶׁה זָכָה וְזִכָּה אֶת־הָרַבִּים זְכוּת הָרַבִּים תָּלוּי בּוֹ שֶׁנֶּאֱמַר צִדְקַת יְיָ עָשָׂה וּמִשְׁפָּטָיו עִם־יִשְׂרָאֵל·יָרָבְעָם בֶּן־נְבָט חָטָא וְהֶחֱטִיא אֶת־הָרַבִּים חֵטְא הָרַבִּים תָּלוּי בּוֹ שֶׁנֶּאֱמַר עַל־חַטֹּאות יָרָבְעָם אֲשֶׁר חָטָא וַאֲשֶׁר הֶחֱטִיא אֶת־יִשְׂרָאֵל :

20. When in a controversy both parties are guided solely by pure motives and seek noble ends (such is the implication of the term לשם שמים), and when both parties seek solely to find the truth, then, of course, only one view will constitute the truth and only one of the two opposing views can and will prevail in practice. But actually, both views will have permanent value because, through the arguments each side has presented, both parties will have served to shed new light on the issue under debate, and will have contributed to the attainment of the proper understanding of the question discussed. They shall be remembered as long as there are men sincerely interested both in the subject of the debate and in the finding of the truth. For such men, retaining an abiding memory of the differences and the attempts on both sides to prove the validity of their views, will study the arguments of both sides thoroughly and repeatedly, thus advancing the cause of the genuine knowledge of truth. Thus, controversies such as those between Hillel and Shammai and between the other *Tannaim* and *Amoraim* have remained a permanent and important component of our Torah and its study.

20. Any controversy with a noble purpose will result in abiding value, but any controversy that has no noble purpose shall not have abiding value. Which controversy was one that had a noble purpose? The controversy between Hillel and Shammai. And which controversy had no noble purpose? The controversy of Korach and his company.

21. He who leads the multitude to righteousness shall have no sin come into his hand, but he who leads the multitude to sin shall not get the opportunity to succeed in his repentance. Moshe was righteous and led the multitude to righteousness. The righteousness of the multitude was ascribed to him forever, as it is said, "He performed the righteousness of *God* and his righteous ordinances remained with Yisrael." Yaravam, the son of Nevat, sinned and led the multitude to sin. The sin of the multitude was ascribed to him forever, as it is said, "Because of the sin of Yaravam who sinned and caused Yisrael to sin."

---

21. He who leads his people to righteousness will be guarded from sin by the grace of God. This could mean that no wrong will be done *through him*, and could also mean that no wrong will be perpetrated *by him*, so that he will always remain a shining example for that community which he himself guided to a life of purity. Thus by virtue of the righteousness which he practiced himself and also enjoined upon Israel to practice, Moses, for instance, remains associated forever with all the acts of righteousness that his people will carry out through all the generations to come. But he who induces a multitude to lead a life of sin will never succeed even in genuinely repenting of his own misdeeds and in seeking to do better. For the first prerequisite for his own genuine repentance is that he must lead back to the good life all those whom he has led astray, and that is certainly impossible. Indeed, the criminal act of inducement to sin goes on and on and continues to fester as a pernicious growth in the midst even of all the generations that come after the one which was originally led astray. We are told in Kings I, 15:30 that the entire dynasty of Jerobeam perished by reason of the criminal seduction perpetrated by its ancestor. All the accounts in the Book of Kings of the transgressions perpetrated by the rulers of the Kingdom of Israel stress that it was the evil example of their ancestor that caused them to sin, and at the very outset (Kings I, 14:15, 16) it is asserted that the seduction committed by Jerobeam will result in the banishment of his people.

כב כָּל־מִי שֶׁיֶּשׁ־בּוֹ שְׁלֹשָׁה דְבָרִים הַלָּלוּ הוּא מִתַּלְמִידָיו שֶׁל־
אַבְרָהָם אָבִינוּ, וּשְׁלֹשָׁה דְבָרִים אֲחֵרִים הוּא מִתַּלְמִידָיו שֶׁל־
בִּלְעָם הָרָשָׁע. עַיִן טוֹבָה וְרוּחַ נְמוּכָה וְנֶפֶשׁ שְׁפָלָה מִתַּלְמִידָיו
שֶׁל־אַבְרָהָם אָבִינוּ. עַיִן רָעָה וְרוּחַ גְּבוֹהָה וְנֶפֶשׁ רְחָבָה מִתַּלְמִידָיו
שֶׁל־בִּלְעָם הָרָשָׁע. מַה בֵּין תַּלְמִידָיו שֶׁל־אַבְרָהָם אָבִינוּ
לְתַלְמִידָיו שֶׁל־בִּלְעָם הָרָשָׁע. תַּלְמִידָיו שֶׁל־אַבְרָהָם אָבִינוּ
אוֹכְלִין בָּעוֹלָם הַזֶּה וְנוֹחֲלִין הָעוֹלָם הַבָּא שֶׁנֶּאֱמַר לְהַנְחִיל
אֹהֲבַי יֵשׁ וְאוֹצְרֹתֵיהֶם אֲמַלֵּא. תַּלְמִידָיו שֶׁל־בִּלְעָם הָרָשָׁע יוֹרְשִׁין
גֵּיהִנֹּם וְיוֹרְדִין לִבְאֵר שַׁחַת שֶׁנֶּאֱמַר וְאַתָּה אֱלֹהִים תּוֹרִדֵם
לִבְאֵר שַׁחַת אַנְשֵׁי דָמִים וּמִרְמָה לֹא־יֶחֱצוּ יְמֵיהֶם וַאֲנִי אֶבְטַח־בָּךְ:

כג יְהוּדָה בֶּן־תֵּימָא אוֹמֵר, הֱוֵה עַז כַּנָּמֵר וְקַל כַּנֶּשֶׁר רָץ
כַּצְּבִי וְגִבּוֹר כָּאֲרִי לַעֲשׂוֹת רְצוֹן אָבִיךָ שֶׁבַּשָּׁמָיִם:

---

22. The life of Abraham was characterized by these virtues: עַיִן טוֹבָה:
he truly loved his fellow-men and therefore he could rejoice without envy or
reserve in their every good fortune; he was modest and he was undemanding.
These qualities immediately came to the fore, when Abraham left his father's
house, and gave up all the pleasures, riches, comforts, and honors of home to
go out into the strange and inhospitable unknown; all in order to advance the
welfare of his fellow-men. They were proven, too, by Abraham's conduct
toward his nephew and his wife, by the practical mercy he showed to wan-
derers whom he did not know, by the battle he waged to aid his ungrateful
nephew, long estranged from him, and by his unselfishness after he had won
the victory. The picture of his long and trial-laden life shows no trace whatever of conduct at variance with these noble traits. In striking contrast to
this, we behold the arrogance, the insatiable ambition and the greed of the
malicious Bileam who was ready to pronounce a curse over an entire people.
We cannot find in Bileam's character sketch even one stroke that might miti-
gate this unsavory picture in the gallery of history. The disciples of Abraham
love their fellow-men, they are modest, humble, utterly untainted by envy.
These sterling qualities not only open for them the portals of bliss in the
world to come, but give them serenity and happiness even here on earth regardless of the lack of material wealth and pleasures and the burden of
trials and privation that life may bring. Their measure of calamities seems

22. He who has these three attributes is among the disciples of Father Avraham, and three other attributes mark the disciples of the lawless Bileam. A good eye, a humble mind and an undemanding soul are the characteristics of the disciples of our Father Avraham. An evil eye, a haughty mind and a demanding soul are the characteristics of the disciples of the lawless Bileam. What difference is there between the lot of the disciples of our Father Avraham and that of the disciples of the lawless Bileam? The disciples of our Father Avraham enjoy this world and inherit the world to come, as it is said, "That I may cause those who love Me to inherit substance, and I shall fill their treasuries." The disciples of the lawless Bileam, on the other hand, inherit Gehinnom and descend into the pit of destruction; for it is said: "You, O *God,* will bring them down into the pit; men of murder and deceit shall not live out [even] half their days, but I will trust in You."

23. Yehudah the son of Tema, said: Be strong as a leopard, light as an eagle, swift as a stag and mighty as a lion to do the will of your Father in Heaven.

---

small in their eyes, and the happiness of others which they create, promote, and observe affords them a source of joy which the disciples of Bileam cannot possibly surmise. As for the disciples of Bileam, their malice, their arrogance and their insatiable greed and ambition not only make it impossible for them to walk upon the road to salvation in the world to come, but also keep them from finding one moment's true contentment, even in the midst of an abundance of riches and pleasures. Any joy, honor or prosperity that comes to others is a bitter drop in their cup of joy and whatever they may already have achieved loses all value in their eyes when they contemplate those of their desires that are still unfulfilled. Hence לא יחצו ימיהם they do not receive a portion in either of the two worlds originally appointed for them, even as they had been for all other men. The world to come is closed to them and the happiness possible in this world is truly lost to them as well.

23. עז — "strong as a leopard" to resist any attempt to lure you away from good and to induce you to do evil. קל—"light as an eagle" so that, leaving all earthly impediments behind you, you may soar up to God. רץ— "swift as a hart" so that you will know neither procrastination nor hesitation in matters of the performance of your duty. גבור "mighty as a lion" to overcome all obstacles, both within and without.

כד הוּא הָיָה אוֹמֵר, עַז פָּנִים לְגֵיהִנָּם וּבוֹשֶׁת פָּנִים לְגַן עֵדֶן:

יְהִי רָצוֹן מִלְּפָנֶיךָ יְיָ אֱלֹהֵינוּ וֵאלֹהֵי אֲבוֹתֵינוּ שֶׁיִּבָּנֶה בֵּית הַמִּקְדָּשׁ בִּמְהֵרָה בְיָמֵינוּ וְתֵן חֶלְקֵנוּ בְּתוֹרָתֶךָ:

כה הוּא הָיָה אוֹמֵר, בֶּן חָמֵשׁ שָׁנִים לַמִּקְרָא בֶּן עֶשֶׂר שָׁנִים לַמִּשְׁנָה בֶּן שְׁלֹשׁ עֶשְׂרֵה לַמִּצְוֹת בֶּן חֲמֵשׁ עֶשְׂרֵה לַתַּלְמוּד בֶּן שְׁמֹנֶה עֶשְׂרֵה לַחֻפָּה בֶּן עֶשְׂרִים לִרְדּוֹף בֶּן שְׁלֹשִׁים לַכֹּחַ בֶּן אַרְבָּעִים לַבִּינָה בֶּן חֲמִשִּׁים לְעֵצָה בֶּן שִׁשִּׁים לְזִקְנָה בֶּן שִׁבְעִים לְשֵׂיבָה בֶּן שְׁמוֹנִים לִגְבוּרָה בֶּן תִּשְׁעִים לָשׁוּחַ בֶּן מֵאָה כְּאִלּוּ מֵת וְעָבַר וּבָטֵל מִן הָעוֹלָם:

כו בֶּן בַּג בַּג אוֹמֵר, הֲפָךְ בָּהּ וַהֲפָךְ בָּהּ דְּכֹלָּא בָהּ וּבָהּ תֶּחֱזֵא וְסִיב וּבְלֵה בָהּ וּמִנַּהּ לָא תָזוּעַ שֶׁאֵין לְךָ מִדָּה טוֹבָה הֵימֶנָּה:

כז בֶּן הֵא הֵא אוֹמֵר, לְפֻם צַעֲרָא אַגְרָא:

רבי חנניא וכו'. קדיש.

---

24. We have read in the Mishna immediately preceding that firmness and defiance against obstacles is praiseworthy when it comes to fulfilling the will of God. But such conduct is not necessarily beneficial in our relationships with our fellowmen and in the attainment of objectives placed at man's own discretion. Here boldness without consideration may easily lead to such impudence, utterly devoid of scruples, as will be conducive only to sure ruin. A certain degree of timidity, on the other hand, will guard a man from many errors and will give rise to prudence, the deliberate weighing of every step to be taken, a virtue that will support and raise the moral value of life in terms of duty fulfilled. יהי רצון : The connection of this prayer with the verses that precede is not quite clear. It may be based on a thought as follows: We have just learned that under the guidance of the Word of God and employed in the service of His Torah even the most differing and mutually contradictory talents and potentialities can be utilized for good, whereas without such guidance, and subordinated to alien endeavors these same qualities would lead to utter ruin. Therefore we now pray that, speedily and soon, we may be permitted to rejoice in the rebuilding of the Sanctuary of the Law and thus in God's complete guidance and that then, every man, each according to his own talents and abilities, may find "his own portion" in the fulfillment of God's Law on earth.

24. He used to say: The impudent is destined for Gehinnom; the shamefaced for the Garden of Eden. May it be Your will, *God* our God, that the Sanctuary be rebuilt speedily in our days and give us our portion in Your Teaching.

25. He used to say: At five years [the age is reached] for [the study of] the Scriptures, at ten for [the study of] the Mishna, at thirteen for the Mitzvoth, at fifteen for [the study of] the Gemarah, at eighteen for marriage, at twenty for the pursuit of the aim [in life], at thirty for strength, at forty for insight, at fifty for counsel; at sixty man attains old age, at seventy, the hoary head; at eighty, extreme old age, at ninety, decline, and at one hundred he is as if he were already dead and gone and departed from this world.

26. Ben Bagbag said: Occupy yourself with it over and over again, for everything is contained in it, and it is through it that your view will attain clarity; grow old and gray with it and depart not from it, for there is no better pursuit for you than the Torah.

27. Ben He-he said: According to the effort is the reward.

---

25. If, as specified in this passage, a boy, by the time he has reached the age of fifteen, has behind him ten years of מקרא, of Bible study, and five of Mishna, he should have become so familiar with the basic truths of Judaism and with the fundamental concepts and requirements of our Law that it should be an easy thing for him to make the transition to the commentaries, reasonings and inferences contained in the Gemarah, the work that "completes" the Torah. After five years spent in the study of the Mishna, no subject contained in the Gemarah should be foreign to the young scholar; by this time he should be able to follow all the debates in the Gemarah with full comprehension and grasp their conclusions with ease. Ah, when shall we see the day when our young people will once again tread the path to spiritual and mental development in accordance with the teaching left us by our wise "fathers"!

It is probable that the term לרדוף, as in צדק תרדוף and רודף שלום, connotes serious, intent *pursuit*, in this case the pursuit of one's daily bread and the concern that should be devoted to the loyal fulfillment of duty. כח denotes the mature strength and energy for toil and labor; בינה refers to the maturing of intellectual powers; עצה implies the mature judgement of things and situations, based on long experience in living, and of the course to be followed in accordance with the dictates of such mature judgement.

26 & 27. Both these verses are in keeping with the way of life outlined in the preceding Mishna, Verse 26 seeks to preclude a possible misinterpretation

כל ישראל וכו'

שָׁנוּ חֲכָמִים בִּלְשׁוֹן הַמִּשְׁנָה בָּרוּךְ שֶׁבָּחַר בָּהֶם וּבְמִשְׁנָתָם:

א רַבִּי מֵאִיר אוֹמֵר, כָּל־הָעוֹסֵק בַּתּוֹרָה לִשְׁמָהּ זוֹכֶה לִדְבָרִים הַרְבֵּה וְלֹא עוֹד אֶלָּא שֶׁכָּל־הָעוֹלָם כֻּלּוֹ כְּדַי הוּא לוֹ, נִקְרָא רֵעַ אָהוּב אוֹהֵב אֶת־הַמָּקוֹם אוֹהֵב אֶת־הַבְּרִיּוֹת מְשַׂמֵּחַ אֶת הַמָּקוֹם מְשַׂמֵּחַ אֶת הַבְּרִיּוֹת וּמַלְבַּשְׁתּוֹ עֲנָוָה וְיִרְאָה וּמַכְשַׁרְתּוֹ לִהְיוֹת צַדִּיק חָסִיד יָשָׁר וְנֶאֱמָן וּמְרַחַקְתּוֹ מִן־הַחֵטְא וּמְקָרַבְתּוֹ לִידֵי זְכוּת וְנֶהֱנִין מִמֶּנּוּ עֵצָה וְתוּשִׁיָּה בִּינָה וּגְבוּרָה שֶׁנֶּאֱמַר לִי עֵצָה וְתוּשִׁיָּה אֲנִי בִינָה לִי גְבוּרָה וְנוֹתֶנֶת לוֹ מַלְכוּת וּמֶמְשָׁלָה וְחִקּוּר דִּין וּמְגַלִּין לוֹ רָזֵי תוֹרָה וְנַעֲשֶׂה כְּמַעְיָן שֶׁאֵינוֹ פוֹסֵק וּכְנָהָר הַמִּתְגַּבֵּר וְהוֹלֵךְ וְהֹוֶה צָנוּעַ וְאֶרֶךְ רוּחַ וּמוֹחֵל עַל־עֶלְבּוֹנוֹ וּמְגַדַּלְתּוֹ וּמְרוֹמַמְתּוֹ עַל־כָּל־הַמַּעֲשִׂים:

---

of the course of study indicated in Verse 25. When it is said that בן חמש למקרא, בן עשר למשנה וכו', we are taught that this does not mean that a boy need study the Scriptures only until he is ten years old, the Mishna only until he is fifteen, that he need study the Gemarah no longer than until his eighteenth or twentieth year, and that thereafter the study of the Torah must yield place to other pursuits. Quite the contrary—it is pointed out here that it is incumbent upon us to occupy ourselves with the Scriptures, as well as with the Mishnah and the Gemarah throughout our lives. We are bidden to return to this sacred pursuit over and over again, for the Torah is the one inexhaustible source of all the knowledge of what is good and true and worthwhile, and the longer and the more faithfully we occupy ourselves with it, the broader and stronger will our power of spiritual vision grow. Therefore let the Torah remain at your side even when you are old and when your energies for all other pursuits have declined, and do not depart from it as long as you live, for you can acquire no greater consecration for your endeavors. Ben He He adds to this overview of the plan for our life's course: It is not the quantitative measure of the moral and spiritual and social goals you have actually achieved that constitutes the true worth of a life's course. It is צערא, the measure of earnest striving, of devoted endeavor, of sacrifices made and privation endured, all for the realization of good purposes such as meet with God's approval that determines the true worth of both a man and his life. For actual success can only come from the hands of God Himself.

The sages taught the following in the style of the Mishna; blessed be He Who chose them and their teaching.

1. Rabbi Meir said: He who occupies himself with the Torah with a pure purpose acquires many things; nay more, he alone would be sufficient for the continued existence of the whole world. He is called friend, beloved; he loves God, he loves [His] creatures, he gladdens God and he gladdens [God's] creatures, and it clothes him in meekness and the fear of God; it enables him to be just, merciful, upright and faithful; it keeps him far from error and will bring him to virtue. Through him men benefit from counsel and sound wisdom, insight and strength, for it is said: "Counsel is mine and sound wisdom; I am insight, mine is strength." It gives him sovereignty and dominion and discerning judgement; the secrets of the Torah are revealed to him, and he becomes like a fountain that never fails, and like a river which constantly gains in vigor, and he remains modest, patient and forgiving of insults, and it makes him great and exalted over all creatures.

CHAPTER VI

The verses contained in this portion do not constitute Mishna but בריית‎, verses which have been preserved "outside" or "apart from" the actual Mishna code; they are written in the style of the Mishna and constitute explanations and supplements to the Mishna passages. ברוך‎, blessed be "He", God, Who chose the Sages and their teaching to labor in His service.

1. To "occupy oneself with תורה לשמה‎" means to study it thoroughly and for one purpose only; that is, to discern from it the will of God, and to do God's will by fulfilling it oneself and teaching it to others. The study of the Torah in this spirit, free of all baser motives and founded on the purest of purposes, will render life, thus guided by the Word of God, rich in blessed attainment and will enable man and his endeavors to reach so high a plane that the entire world will derive satisfaction from him. If in all the course of its development, there will come forth upon earth even only one single person of this type, then the world will not have existed in vain. Such a person is "כדאי‎" of this world.

But particularly and especially it is spiritual and moral character attainments that the pure study of the Torah affords. — נקרא רע‎: The Torah describes men in their relationship to each other in pure conformity with its Law as רע‎, implying that in this ideal situation each man offers himself to

ג אָמַר רַבִּי יְהוֹשֻׁעַ בֶּן־לֵוִי, בְּכָל־יוֹם וָיוֹם בַּת־קוֹל יוֹצֵאת
מֵהַר חוֹרֵב וּמַכְרֶזֶת וְאוֹמֶרֶת אוֹי לָהֶם לַבְּרִיּוֹת מֵעֶלְבּוֹנָהּ שֶׁל־
תּוֹרָה, שֶׁכָּל־מִי שֶׁאֵינוֹ עוֹסֵק בַּתּוֹרָה נִקְרָא נָזוּף שֶׁנֶּאֱמַר נֶזֶם
זָהָב בְּאַף חֲזִיר אִשָּׁה יָפָה וְסָרַת טָעַם: וְאוֹמֵר, וְהַלֻּחֹת מַעֲשֵׂה
אֱלֹהִים הֵמָּה וְהַמִּכְתָּב מִכְתַּב אֱלֹהִים הוּא חָרוּת עַל־הַלֻּחֹת, אַל־
תִּקְרָא חָרוּת אֶלָּא חֵרוּת שֶׁאֵין לְךָ בֶּן־חוֹרִין אֶלָּא מִי שֶׁעוֹסֵק
בְּתַלְמוּד תּוֹרָה וְכָל־מִי שֶׁעוֹסֵק בְּתַלְמוּד תּוֹרָה הֲרֵי זֶה מִתְעַלֶּה
שֶׁנֶּאֱמַר וּמִמַּתָּנָה נַחֲלִיאֵל וּמִנַּחֲלִיאֵל בָּמוֹת:

the other as a "pasture", devoting himself to the "satisfaction" of the other's needs and finding the satisfaction of his own in the welfare and prosperity of the others. Only the pure understanding and fulfillment of the Torah can endow man with such an attitude to his brothers. ומלבשתו: it invests him with ענוה and יראה that is, it makes ענוה and יראה; be those qualities which, like a garment, cling to his personality as inalienable companions. צדיק וחסיד ישר נאמן and נאמן complement the character of the צדיק and חסיד. His צדקות and his חסידות are not dependent on vague, unstable moods that can easily transgress the boundary of what is right. The חסידות and צדקות that are based upon the clear conceptual truths of the Torah are נאמן; and ישר they do not deviate from the straight path and remain steadfast forever. Since they will be no different tomorrow from what they were today they will guard man from error and bring him closer to moral perfection. ונהגין His fellow-men, too, will benefit from his spiritual and moral qualities; therefore they will entrust him with the guidance, the fashioning and the leadership of their affairs even as they would a king, and they will obtain their decisions in matters of justice from his insight and his conscientiousness. ומגלין It is only through such practical activation and application of his Torah knowledge in real-life situations that the inner meaning of God's Law will truly lie revealed before him, and the fountain and the stream of his mental and spiritual talents will grow in vigor to dominate ever-widening territory. והיה (this is the version of our Mishna according to יעב״ץ) and nevertheless he remains צנוע. He prefers to remain modestly retiring; he does not strut about, nor does he glory in the wealth of his accomplishments, and it is on acount of this modesty and humility that the Torah will make him great and raise him above all of his fellow-creatures.

2. The Revelation on Mount Horeb has not as yet attained its ultimate goal among men. As long as there are still men who will not recognize the true

2. Rabbi Yehoshua ben Levi, said: Day after day a daughter-voice goes forth from Mount Horeb proclaiming these words: "Woe to them, to mankind, for their disregard of the Torah" for whoever does not labor in the Torah is called "rebuked"; for it is said: "A golden ring in a swine's snout; a beautiful woman and yet foolish." And it is said, "The Tablets are the works of God and the writing is the writing of God, *charut*, engraved, upon the Tablets." Read not *charut* (engraved) but *cherut* (meaning "freedom"), for man is never more free than when he occupies himself with the study of the Torah, and he who occupies himself with the study of the Torah will be exalted, for it is said: "From *Mattanah* (meaning "gift of God") to *Nachaliel* (meaning "inheritance of God"), and from Nachaliel to *Bamoth* (meaning "the high place").

---

worth of the Teaching and Law thus revealed, and who will not employ it for the spiritual and moral perfection and sanctification of both the inner life and their outward actions, Mount Sinai will stand as a silent rebuke, as it were, before mankind, and without cease a call resounds from Horeb, saying, "It is not the Torah but only man that will suffer loss and distress because he has despised and insulted the Torah." נזיפה denotes the first degree of "banishment" such as occurs when a man of high spiritual and moral plane dismisses from his presence as unworthy a person guilty of reprehensible conduct. In quite the same manner a person who, though he has received the revealed Word of God, has not allowed it to influence his physical and spiritual life for his ennoblement and betterment is unworthy of being near God and is therefore sent away from His presence. Because it is so contrary to the ideal set forth in the Divine Teaching he has received, his crude and ignoble character, unchanged by the Word of God, is unworthy of God's holy Presence. It is as offensive as a woman whose body is beautiful but whose mind and morals are ugly and whose spiritual crudity and moral turpitude are all the more repulsive and obnoxious because of her physical beauty. For physical beauty is a gift which should serve as constant admonition to its possessor, of the spiritual and moral beauty and harmony after which he should strive with all his soul and spirit. Since physical beauty thus suggests spiritual and moral grace and hence holds attraction for those who look upon it, the lack of such spiritual and moral qualities is all the more repugnant. And all who behold this creature will say: "Alas for the beautiful body, even as for the golden ring which adorns a swine and which the beast heedlessly buries in the filth."

Even as the Torah ennobles us, so a truly devoted study of it also makes us free, free from error, free from the temptations of physical lusts and

ג הַלּוֹמֵד מֵחֲבֵרוֹ פֶּרֶק אֶחָד אוֹ הֲלָכָה אַחַת אוֹ פָסוּק אֶחָד אוֹ
דִבּוּר אֶחָד אוֹ אֲפִילוּ אוֹת אַחַת צָרִיךְ לִנְהָג בּוֹ כָבוֹד, שֶׁכֵּן
מָצִינוּ בְּדָוִד מֶלֶךְ יִשְׂרָאֵל שֶׁלֹּא לָמַד מֵאֲחִיתֹפֶל אֶלָּא שְׁנֵי
דְבָרִים בִּלְבָד קְרָאוֹ רַבּוֹ אַלוּפוֹ וּמְיֻדָעוֹ שֶׁנֶּאֱמַר וְאַתָּה אֱנוֹשׁ
כְּעֶרְכִּי אַלוּפִי וּמְיֻדָעִי: וַהֲלֹא דְבָרִים קַל וָחֹמֶר, וּמַה דָּוִד מֶלֶךְ
יִשְׂרָאֵל שֶׁלֹּא לָמַד מֵאֲחִיתֹפֶל אֶלָּא שְׁנֵי דְבָרִים בִּלְבָד קְרָאוֹ
רַבּוֹ אַלוּפוֹ וּמְיֻדָעוֹ, הַלּוֹמֵד מֵחֲבֵרוֹ פֶּרֶק אֶחָד אוֹ הֲלָכָה אַחַת
אוֹ פָסוּק אֶחָד אוֹ דִבּוּר אֶחָד אוֹ אֲפִילוּ אוֹת אַחַת עַל-אַחַת
בַּמָּה וְכַמָּה שֶׁצָּרִיךְ לִנְהָג בּוֹ כָבוֹד • וְאֵין כָבוֹד אֶלָּא תוֹרָה
שֶׁנֶּאֱמַר כָּבוֹד חֲכָמִים יִנְחָלוּ, וּתְמִימִים יִנְחֲלוּ טוֹב • וְאֵין טוֹב
אֶלָּא תוֹרָה שֶׁנֶּאֱמַר כִּי לֶקַח טוֹב נָתַתִּי לָכֶם תּוֹרָתִי אַל-תַּעֲזֹבוּ:

ד כָּךְ הִיא דַּרְכָּהּ שֶׁל-תּוֹרָה, פַּת בְּמֶלַח תֹּאכֵל וּמַיִם בִּמְשׂוּרָה

---

desires and free from the crushing and degrading power of the multitude of
worries and troubles of daily living. The Sages derived this truth from the
etymological reinterpretation of חרות to imply חרות, the more so since, according to tradition, the writing engraved through the stone Tablets itself, as in
the (character of the suspension of the inner parts of the letters ס, ם,) and the
exemplified support of earthly lives that is free of all external bands and is
borne only by the power of God (ם וסמך שבלוחות בנס הם עומדין). The place names
מתנה, נחליאל, במות are taken from the song which Israel sang of the Well
(Num. 21:19) and allude to the stations of Miriam's Well which accompanied our forefathers on their journey through the wilderness. These place
names are apt allegorical designations for the stations of learning and development through which we will pass if we will let ourselves be guided by the
Well of God's Torah on our earthly pilgrimage and if we will draw from it the
life-giving waters of spiritual and moral ennoblement. We are to accept the
Torah as מתנה "the gift of God". Then, once we allow it to penetrate our
inmost being through and through, it will become our inalienable "Godly
inheritance" and will lead us on to those "high places" toward which all on
earth may aspire.

3. The proper understanding of the Word of God is of such great importance; upon it depends to such great extent whether or not we can give proper
direction to our thoughts, our endeavors and our achievements; that we must

3. He who learns from his fellow-man even one chapter, one rule, one verse, one expression or even one single letter, must pay him honor. Thus we find in the case of David, the King of Israel, who learned only two things from Achitophel and yet he called him his master, his guide and his confidant. For it is said: "You are a man equal to me; you are my guide and my confidant." Now we may infer [as follows]: If David, the King of Israel, who had learned only two things from Achitophel, called him his teacher, his guide and his familiar friend, how much more ought one who learns from his fellow one chapter, one rule, one verse, one expression or even only one single letter, to pay him honor? And honor is inherent only in the Torah, for it is said, "The wise ones will inherit honor and that which is good will be inherited by those who are observant [of the Torah]." Only the Torah is truly good, for it is said, "I have given you a good Teaching, forsake not My Torah."

4. This is the way of the Torah: To eat bread with salt, to drink water by measure, to sleep upon the ground and live a life of hardship,

---

honor as our greatest benefactor any man who has contributed to our better understanding of the Torah, regardless of how small his contribution may seem. The nature of our Hebrew language is such that the manner in which we interpret even one single letter can be of decisive importance in our understanding of the whole. In Hebrew, particles, prepositions and conjunctions are represented by one single letter; likewise, tense and mood, number, gender of the object, and so forth, are indicated by changes in individual letters. Thus the connotation of such words in a sentence and its context can often be determined only by the correct interpretation of one specific letter. We are told that Achitophel taught David just two things—the importance of studying the Torah with a group, and the importance of worshipping as a congregation. This is indicated in Psalm 55:15 where David says of Achitophel: אשר יחדו נמתיק סוד בבית אלהים נהלך ברגש "Together we savored the sweetness of delving into the inmost meaning of the Torah, and we walked in the House of God in the midst of the teeming multitude." It is the Torah that holds our true human dignity and our true salvation. Therefore אין כבוד ואין טוב אלא תורה.

4. Verse 3 told of the honor and the happiness which can be won through constant diligent toil in the Torah. This verse is added by way of amendment, lest you should come to believe that the kind of honor and happiness that can be gained upon the path of Torah must always be visible and tangible.

תִּשְׁתֶּה וְעַל הָאָרֶץ תִּישָׁן וְחַיֵּי צַעַר תִּחְיֶה וּבַתּוֹרָה אַתָּה עָמֵל
אִם־אַתָּה עֹשֶׂה כֵּן אַשְׁרֶיךָ וְטוֹב לָךְ אַשְׁרֶיךָ בָּעוֹלָם הַזֶּה וְטוֹב
לָךְ לָעוֹלָם הַבָּא :

ה אַל־תְּבַקֵּשׁ גְּדֻלָּה לְעַצְמָךְ וְאַל־תַּחְמוֹד כָּבוֹד · יוֹתֵר מִלִּמּוּדָךְ
עֲשֵׂה וְאַל־תִּתְאַוֶּה לְשֻׁלְחָנָם שֶׁל־מְלָכִים שֶׁשֻּׁלְחָנְךָ גָּדוֹל
מִשֻּׁלְחָנָם וְכִתְרְךָ גָּדוֹל מִכִּתְרָם וְנֶאֱמָן הוּא בַּעַל מְלַאכְתְּךָ
שֶׁיְּשַׁלֶּם לָךְ שְׂכַר פְּעֻלָּתֶךָ :

י גְּדוֹלָה תוֹרָה יוֹתֵר מִן־הַכְּהֻנָּה וּמִן־הַמַּלְכוּת · שֶׁהַמַּלְכוּת
נִקְנִית בִּשְׁלֹשִׁים מַעֲלוֹת וְהַכְּהֻנָּה בְּעֶשְׂרִים וְאַרְבַּע, וְהַתּוֹרָה
נִקְנִית בְּאַרְבָּעִים וּשְׁמוֹנָה דְבָרִים · וְאֵלּוּ הֵן, בְּתַלְמוּד, בִּשְׁמִיעַת
הָאֹזֶן, בַּעֲרִיכַת שְׂפָתַיִם, בְּבִינַת הַלֵּב בְּשִׂכְלוּל הַלֵּב, בְּאֵימָה,
בְּיִרְאָה, בַּעֲנָוָה, בְּשִׂמְחָה, (בטהרה) בְּשִׁמּוּשׁ חֲכָמִים, בְּדִבּוּק

The true power inherent in the Torah lies in the very fact that it can teach its true disciples readily and serenely to forego all outward honor and prosperity and that it permits them to find and enjoy in day-to-day living such happiness and bliss which, in the midst of privation and renunciation, can turn life on earth into a wellspring of the purest joy and imbue them with confidence in the future bliss of the world to come.

5. Seek recognition not for your own person but solely for the sacred cause for which you live and strive. Do not allow yourself to become envious when others are honored while you stand aside unnoticed. Do not devote yourself only to theoretical study, but do and accomplish more than you have learned. If you so live, then your "table"—that which life offers you and with which you gird yourself for service to your life's duty—will be far more opulent than even the festive boards of kings. Then your study and your deeds will have influence and dignity far greater even than the sovereign power of kings, and the Employer in Whose service you study and labor will let you find the reward for your selfless loyalty.

6. In Chapter 4, Verse 13 we are told that there are three crowns; the crown of Torah, that of priesthood and that of kingship. In this passage these three crowns are compared with one another with respect to דברים שנקנין בם.

and to study the Torah diligently all the while. If you do this, then you will be happy and it shall be well with you; you will be happy in this life and it shall be well with you in the world to come.

5. Seek not greatness for yourself and strive not after honor; let your works exceed your learning and crave not after the tables of kings; for your table is greater than theirs and your crown is greater than their crowns, and your Employer is faithful to pay you the reward for your work.

6. The Torah is greater than priesthood and kingship, for while kingship is acquired by thirty prerogatives, and the priesthood by twenty-four, the Torah is acquired by forty-eight qualifications. And these are they: by study, by proper listening, by ordered speech, by understanding, by pondering over what one has understood, by earnestness, by reverence, by modesty, by joy, (by purity), by association with wise men, by communion with colleagues, by discussion

---

Now שנקנין בם cannot be given the same interpretation in connection with all the three crowns. Priesthood, for example, can never be "acquired"; it is a title which can be inherited by birth only. Kingship, too, is generally hereditary; if only the son will fill his father's place in the genuine, conscientious fear of God, ממלא מקומו ביראה, the majesty of kingship will automatically pass from father to son. Actually, the thirty and twenty-four מעלות which are mentioned here in connection with מלכות and כהונה respectively, (for an enumeration of those of kingship see Chapter 9 of the First Book of Samuel, and Sanhedrin 18; for those of priesthood, Chapter 18 of the Book of Numbers) are not moral or spiritual virtues, but *prerogatives* that are part of the office of kingship and priesthood. They are not מעלות by means of which these titles can be acquired, but qualities which are associated with them and which are acquired together with the office. The forty-eight דברים enumerated here in connection with the תורה, however, are not prerogatives associated with the "crown" which Torah affords, but "qualifications", moral and spiritual talents and virtues, which he who strives after the crown of the Torah must acquire and employ through diligent labor upon his own personality before he can attain to the goal of the Torah. These forty-eight attributes are not *gifts* which are acquired together with the Torah, but *means* through which alone it is possible to acquire the crown of the Torah. If one wishes one may also logically say that all the moral and spiritual attributes named here are indeed acquired simultaneously with the Torah because, in fact, it is possible to acquire the Torah only if one also possesses these virtues. — בלימוד: by *teaching*. Personal guidance and instruction by a teacher are essential for

חֲבֵרִים, בְּפִלְפּוּל הַתַּלְמִידִים, בְּיִשּׁוּב, בְּמִקְרָא, בְּמִשְׁנָה, בְּמִעוּט
סְחוֹרָה, בְּמִעוּט דֶּרֶךְ אֶרֶץ, בְּמִעוּט תַּעֲנוּג, בְּמִעוּט שֵׁנָה, בְּמִעוּט
שִׂיחָה, בְּמִעוּט שְׂחוֹק, בְּאֶרֶךְ אַפַּיִם, בְּלֶב־טוֹב, בֶּאֱמוּנַת חֲכָמִים,
בְּקַבָּלַת הַיִּסּוּרִין, הַמַּכִּיר אֶת־מְקוֹמוֹ, וְהַשָּׂמֵחַ בְּחֶלְקוֹ, וְהָעֹשֶׂה
סְיָג לִדְבָרָיו, וְאֵינוֹ מַחֲזִיק טוֹבָה לְעַצְמוֹ, אָהוּב, אוֹהֵב אֶת־

---

knowledge and understanding of the Torah. Even though the Oral Tradition has been put down in writing, it still cannot be passed on properly without also being taught by the spoken word. בשמיעת אזן : Proper, accurate and thorough *listening* is the first demand made on the learner. Such intent and accurate listening precludes any carelessness, inattention or distraction by other things. בעריכת שפתים : The importance of the proper, accurate and logical *enunciation* and *verbalization* of what has been learned cannot be overestimated, for such verbalization serves not only as a test of the thought but also as a means for impressing and retaining in the mind the subject matter thus thought over. That which we cannot put into words clearly and distinctly we cannot possibly know with any degree of clarity; verbalization will clarify our thinking and help to fix permanently in our minds the subject of our thinking. בכונת הלב : by *attention;* literally, "by the *intention* of the heart". The student must be anxious truly to learn that which he must study; he must apply all of his mental power to both the learning and the retention of the material to be studied. בבינת הלב : However, he must not be content merely to absorb the knowledge exactly as it was presented to him; he must make himself comprehend and understand that which the teacher has told him; and digest it mentally. באימה ביראה : At the same time, though, he must ever be aware of the sacred meaning of the subject and also of the medium through which he acquires his knowledge. The source from which he is to draw nourishment for his mind so that he may arrange all of the thoughts, desires and achievements of his life in accordance with the will of God, is Divine revelation, and the Written and Oral Tradition which open to him the wellsprings of wisdom, are Divinely appointed media for this purpose. Once he realizes all this, he will be constantly and anxiously on guard lest, by overestimating his mental capacities and by impertinent disregard of his inadequacies, he should violate the dignity of the sacred subject and its bearers and thus block his own path to true wisdom. As he advances in his studies, he will be imbued with ever growing awe and reverence for both the Torah and its teachers. Thus, even while studying, he will acquire ענוה, modesty, that loftiest of virtues which will remain his most faithful guard and protection against any misstep and error on the path to wisdom and practical observance. בשמחה : According to the teaching of our Sages there is no greater

with students, by prudence, by knowledge of the Scriptures and of the Mishna; by moderation in business activity, in civic affairs, in physical pleasure, in sleep, in conversation, and in jest; by patience, by good-naturedness, by trust in the Sages, and by acceptance of sufferings. [A person such as] he knows his place, he rejoices in his portion, he puts a fence to his words, he does not claim merit for

---

means for spiritual progress and elevation than that serenity and joy of the spirit which will cause a man to rejoice in life with all its tasks and burdens. It is that שמחה של מצוה which will make him resolve all of life with its manifold aspects and changing situations into the one thought of מצוה, and thus acquire that joyful vitality which nothing can quench or subdue. The Sages teach us that the mood that makes man worthy and capable of attaining the nearness of the Divine Spirit is not: עצלות עצבות שחוק קלות ראש ודברים בטלים, neither apathy nor sadness; nor jest, levity or aimless talk, but שמחה של מצוה (Pesachim 117a). Thus a disciple of Torah wisdom must have not only אימה יראה וענוה but also שמחה which will make him rejoice in his every spiritual advance in his understanding of the Word of God and which will keep his spirit alert and quick for the arduous climb upon the steep road to wisdom. בשמוש חכמים בדבוק חברים בפלפל תלמידים: Isolation is incompatible with Jewish knowledge; it is only by association with living sages, in close communion with associates, and the by clarity of thought and judgment that can be attained by teaching it to disciples that the knowledge of Torah can be nurtured and promoted. בישוב, by calm and prudence. The joy in spiritual perception must not lead the student to quick, premature grasping, and to rash thoughts and conclusions, without first having taken the time to study every aspect of the subject and prudently testing the premises. Calm and prudent learning is the mother of true and thorough knowledge. במקרא במשנה: It would seem that the quality of ישוב was intentionally placed just before the knowledge of מקרא and משנה; מקרא and משנה both precede the Talmud and constitute its basis. Now ישוב, such prudent, methodical study as will lead to the desired goal will not simply guard against omitting these preliminary disciplines but will, in fact, constantly pursue the cultivation of these preliminaries even as it advances to more complex subject matter. במיעוט שנה: In order to gain time for his studies, he who is desirous of acquiring Torah wisdom must limit his hours of sleep to the minimum that is necessary for the preservation of his health. במיעוט שיחה: Nor must he waste his time on idle, superfluous chatter; generally speaking, the great Masters of our wisdom deem excessive talk detrimental to the needed earnestness and spiritual composure essential for study. (see Chapter 1, Verse 17). במיעוט סחורה The Mishna presumes that anyone who is anxious to acquire Torah wisdom does not engage in this high pursuit for material gain, but has another source of livelihood to which he

הַמָּקוֹם, אוֹהֵב אֶת־הַבְּרִיּוֹת, אוֹהֵב אֶת־הַצְּדָקוֹת, אוֹהֵב אֶת־
הַמֵּישָׁרִים, אוֹהֵב אֶת הַתּוֹכָחוֹת, וּמִתְרַחֵק מִן־הַכָּבוֹד, וְלֹא־מֵגִיס
לִבּוֹ בְּתַלְמוּדוֹ, וְאֵינוֹ שָׂמֵחַ בְּהוֹרָאָה, נוֹשֵׂא בְעוֹל עִם־חֲבֵרוֹ,
וּמַכְרִיעוֹ לְכַף זְכוּת, וּמַעֲמִידוֹ עַל־הָאֱמֶת, וּמַעֲמִידוֹ עַל־הַשָּׁלוֹם

---

must of necessity devote a certain amount of time and activity. But if he is to attain the prize of knowledge then he must restrict his business activities, too, to a minimum. This limitation should teach him, in the first place, gladly to forego שחוק and תענוג, sport and luxury. במיעוט דרך ארץ: All of the earthly life, both individual and communal, constitutes the subject of the Torah's wisdom, and the Torah seeks to teach us to view and arrange all human affairs on earth in the light of the Teaching of God. Therefore active participation in civic and communal endeavors is not only a duty which must not be neglected but actually is a contribution of no mean significance to the practical knowledge required for this wisdom. Nevertheless, moderation is essential even in this aspect of living if time, mental clarity and emotional calm are to be preserved for the cultivation of the Torah's wisdom. בארך אפים: He who is quick to anger will find that, in his inevitable dealings with others, he will lose the calm and composure which he should bring to his studies. ארך אפים calm, persevering patience not only in our approach to the subject matter itself but also in our relationships with our teachers, with our companions in the search for knowledge, and with the disciples whom we, in turn, teach—is a virtue not to be understimated in our Torah living and in the pursuit of Torah knowledge. לב טוב: a "good" heart, one to which envy, jealousy and hate can gain no access, leaves both mind and spirit free for one's own complete immersion in the task of seeking knowledge, and is beneficial in no small measure also to our associations with our fellow-students. He who has a "good" heart will rejoice in the spiritual achievements of his companions in the search for knowledge; he will gladly and appreciatively add them to his own store of learning and will not allow carping envy to obscure for him the knowledge and acknowledgement of those facts of truth and right that were discovered and uttered by others. באמונת חכמים. Original, creative activity is most enticing for a mentally gifted and eager disciple of any science, but it may well lead him to depart from the path of truth. For all that, a wisdom such as ours which has been handed down by transmission does indeed offer extensive opportunities and an inexhaustible source for creative mental activity, both for retrospective research into the motives behind the given facts and for the development of deductions to elaborate upon this basic data. However, our wisdom has at its side most effective and corrective safeguards against all error in these endeavors. These are the actual content

his achievements, he is loved, he loves God, loves men, loves kindness, loves rectitude, and loves reproof; he keeps himself far from
honor, he does not feel arrogantly of his learning, he does not delight
in handing down decisions, he shares the burden of his fellow-man
and tends to judge him favorably; he teaches him the viewpoint of
truth and teaches him the position of peace; he engages in mature

---

of the Torah as handed down by transmission, the transmitted canons governing
inquiry, the exemplary precedents established by the bearers and communi-
cators of our tradition, and אמונת חכמים; faithful adherence to the tradition,
the teaching and the example left us by those men whom we rightly call our
חכמים. The measuring and testing of the results of our own thinking against
the standard of the truths they have taught and championed will keep our
own thinking also in the paths of truth. בקבלת יסורין: According to our
Sages, suffering is part of the course by means of which God trains both
mind and spirit for the knowledge and fulfillment of His Teaching. Acceptance and utilization for our spiritual and moral enlightenment of those sufferings that are inseparably a part of our Jewish living, as well as of those
which are specifically ordained by Divine Providence is an important part of
the Torah student's task. Instead of allowing those sufferings to alienate him
from the study of the Torah, it is his duty in the midst of distress to devote
himself all the more fervently to it. המכיר את מקומו: יעב״ץ believes that this
change in construction (we read here not בשמחה בחלקו, בהכרת מקומו but
השמח בחלקו, המכיר את מקומו etc.) indicates that the traits named here and
thereafter are those qualities which will be acquired through the cultivation
of all those virtues enumerated before. המכיר את מקומו: He knows his place
in the field of knowledge; he neither overestimates his abilities nor boasts of
them. He knows the spiritual and moral demands which knowledge makes of
him; he knows the inadequacy of what he has achieved thus far; he does not
push himself forward but remains humble and modest. והשמח בחלקו: Even as
he is content with that portion of earthly goods that has been given him, so
it is in the field of striving for knowledge; he rejoices in the modest measure
of intellectual talent that has been granted him. Though he is fully aware that
he must stand back in favor of others who are far more gifted than he is,
he derives satisfaction from the knowledge that he has faithfully employed
his modest abilities for the advancement of his skills and learning, for he
knows that his Father in Heaven evaluates the achievements of His children
solely in terms of the extent to which they have made good use of the faculties with which He has endowed them. והעושה סיג לדבריו: This modest self-
comprehension shows also in his speech. He will not force his own views
on others; and while he does not restrain himself from voicing his convictions
when outspokenness is fitting and proper, he will qualify all his utterances

וּמִתְיַשֵּׁב לִבּוֹ בְּתַלְמוּדוֹ שׁוֹאֵל וּמֵשִׁיב שׁוֹמֵעַ וּמוֹסִיף, הַלּוֹמֵד עַל
מְנָת לְלַמֵּד, וְהַלּוֹמֵד עַל־מְנָת לַעֲשׂוֹת, הַמַּחְכִּים אֶת־רַבּוֹ, וְהַמְכַוֵּן
אֶת־שְׁמוּעָתוֹ, וְהָאוֹמֵר דָּבָר בְּשֵׁם אוֹמְרוֹ ‧ הָא לָמָדְתָּ כָּל־הָאוֹמֵר
דָּבָר בְּשֵׁם אוֹמְרוֹ מֵבִיא גְאֻלָּה לָעוֹלָם שֶׁנֶּאֱמַר וַתֹּאמֶר אֶסְתֵּר
לַמֶּלֶךְ בְּשֵׁם מָרְדֳּכָי:

---

with the reservation that they are true only to the best of his knowledge.
יאינו מחזיק טובה לעצמו. Nor will such good as he may have achieved in the field
of knowledge and of life fill him with self-praise. He knows how much of
his attainments he owes to favorable circumstances and influences which were
not of his own making but had been placed into his path by the love of Divine
providence. He knows how dependent he has ever been upon God's help in
everything he has ever done and that therefore he can take credit for nothing
more than, at best, his good intention. Knowing all this, he will view whatever
he may have achieved in his life with no other emotion but humility.

אהוב אוהב את המקום אוהב את הבריות: Nothing is more suited to endear a
man to both God and his fellows and to fill him, in turn, with love for God
and mankind, than the study of Jewish wisdom. A true disciple of the knowledge of Torah will first apply and realize in his own person the tasks and
requirements with which his studies deal and to the profound understanding
of which he devotes his soul and spirit. In this manner his own personality
will be ennobled to such an extent that he will gain the love of his fellow-men
without ever seeking it. Moreover, since his wisdom leads him to view all of
life on earth and all the human affairs and relationships taking place there
from the one vantage point of nearness to God and of Divine approval, his
heart will go out, unbidden, to God. And in this great love of God he will
include all men as well, for after all, he knows that mankind is included in
God's purpose and is one of the creations in which God delights. אוהב את
הצדקות אוהב את המישרים These are two principal concepts within whose frame-
work all his knowledge moves: Firstly, the concept of that which is due both
men and circumstances in accordance with the claims inherent in them, or
that which is claimed for them by the will of God. These demands are all
included in the definitions of צדקה in the broadest sense of the word. Secondly,
there is that which, aside from the men and circumstances which it affects,
befits us and is therefore in keeping with the nature and purpose of him
who discharges the obligation. These attitudes and obligations are defined
by the term מישרים.

A true disciple of Torah study loves right, duty and fairness and will
defend them wherever he may go. אוהב את התוכחות Since his ultimate goal
is his own personal moral ennoblement and improvement—which is nothing

reflection when studying; he asks and answers, he listens and adds to his learning. He studies in order to teach and he studies in order to practice; he promotes the wisdom of his teacher; he grasps and retains accurately what has been handed down to him by transmission, and what he has heard of others he will quote in the name of him of whom he has heard it. For so you have learned: He who quotes something in the name of the person who said it brings deliverance to the world. For it is said: "And Esther said to the King in the name of Mordechai."

---

else but the practical fulfillment of the ideals taught him by his studies—he will not be angry with him who will point out to him his errors and faults but will instead thank him with all his heart and view him as his greatest benefactor. ומתרחק מן הכבוד His inner life is so profound, he knows so well how far he still is from true perfection in every respect, he knows the dangerous pitfalls, hindering all advancement, that are inherent in honor and public recognition; therefore he will seek to keep outward honor and recognition as far from himself as he can ואינו שמח בהוראה ולא מגיס לבו בתלמודו This modest opinion of his own mental and spiritual worth will keep him from conceit with regard to his wisdom, and it will guard him, too, from seeking the opportunity to propound his own views and opinions by way of a decision unless it is necessary and required by duty that he do so. נושא בעול עם חברו ומכריעו לכף זכות ומעמידו על האמת ומעמידו על השלום : Even as he seeks to ease his neighbor's burdens in daily living, so, too, he will seek to render assistance to every fellow-seeker of knowledge. He will help ease for him the task of learning and the ways of study; he will seek to give direction to the other's tentative questing so that he will choose the good path, and to strengthen his resolve so that he may champion the cause of truth and peace. ומתישב לבי בתלמודו שואל ומשיב שומע ומוסיף Even once he has attained mastery in his studies, he will preserve for the rest of his life those virtues which he had acquired in his early student days. He will remain prudent and will continue to strive after accuracy in his knowledge; he will remain in close touch with teachers and fellow students, exchanging questions and answers in order to clarify and consolidate his own understanding; he endeavors at all times to enrich his own knowledge by listening to the opinions of others. הלומד על מנת ללמד והלומד על מנת לעשות המחכים את רבו והמכוון את שמועתו והאומר דבר בשם אומרו : Even now that he himself is a master, he continues to study with a view to both teaching and practice; he seeks knowledge from others and those who supply it gain knowledge from him in turn. He is careful to absorb and repeat accurately whatever he has heard from others and he will never pass off as his own that which others have told him.

ז גְּדוֹלָה תּוֹרָה שֶׁהִיא נוֹתֶנֶת חַיִּים לְעוֹשֶׂיהָ בָּעוֹלָם הַזֶּה
וּבָעוֹלָם הַבָּא, שֶׁנֶּאֱמַר כִּי־חַיִּים הֵם לְמוֹצְאֵיהֶם וּלְכָל־בְּשָׂרוֹ
מַרְפֵּא: וְאוֹמֵר רִפְאוּת תְּהִי לְשָׁרֶּךָ וְשִׁקּוּי לְעַצְמוֹתֶיךָ:
וְאוֹמֵר עֵץ־חַיִּים הִיא לַמַּחֲזִיקִים בָּהּ וְתֹמְכֶיהָ מְאֻשָּׁר: וְאוֹמֵר
כִּי לִוְיַת חֵן הֵם לְרֹאשֶׁךָ וַעֲנָקִים לְגַרְגְּרֹתֶיךָ: וְאוֹמֵר תִּתֵּן לְרֹאשֶׁךָ
לִוְיַת־חֵן עֲטֶרֶת תִּפְאֶרֶת תְּמַגְּנֶךָ: וְאוֹמֵר כִּי בִי יִרְבּוּ יָמֶיךָ
וְיוֹסִיפוּ לְךָ שְׁנוֹת חַיִּים: וְאוֹמֵר אֹרֶךְ יָמִים בִּימִינָהּ בִּשְׂמֹאולָהּ
עֹשֶׁר וְכָבוֹד: וְאוֹמֵר כִּי אֹרֶךְ יָמִים וּשְׁנוֹת חַיִּים וְשָׁלוֹם יוֹסִיפוּ לָךְ:

ח רַבִּי שִׁמְעוֹן בֶּן־יְהוּדָה מִשֵּׁם רַבִּי שִׁמְעוֹן בֶּן־יוֹחַאי אוֹמֵר,
הַנּוֹי וְהַכֹּחַ וְהָעֹשֶׁר וְהַכָּבוֹד וְהַחָכְמָה וְהַזִּקְנָה וְהַשֵּׂיבָה וְהַבָּנִים
נָאֶה לַצַּדִּיקִים וְנָאֶה לָעוֹלָם, שֶׁנֶּאֱמַר עֲטֶרֶת תִּפְאֶרֶת שֵׂיבָה

---

7. The fulfillment of the precepts of the Torah—and this includes both study in theory and fulfillment in practice—affords life in this world as well as in the next. Its mandates enable every aspect of man's nature to achieve that growth and activation which is their destiny. In this manner every moment of his existence here below achieves its full value and thus becomes true living, and even the most fleeting moment will acquire permanent and eternal significance. Such is the greatness of the Teaching of God. הם "They", the words themselves and not just the consequences of their fulfillment, are life itself to all those whom they can reach. Every human spirit which reflects upon the Word of God and thinks it through with care, will come alive, and every human body that musters its strength for this purpose will become healthy. רפאות תהי The fulfillment of the precepts of the Teaching of God will guard man's physical organs from physical decline and will keep the marrow in his bones strong and sound. עץ חיים : By giving us the Torah, the Lord has given us once again a "Tree of Life"; wherever we will plant and nurture it, it will transform our surroundings, wherever they may be, into a new Paradise. In the original Garden of Eden, the "Tree of Life" and the "Tree of Knowledge" were two separate plants; therefore we lost the "Tree of Life" because of the fruits of the "Tree of Knowledge". But in the Torah the "Tree of Life" and the "Tree of Knowledge" are one and the same, and hence both, inseparable, are the inalienable possession of him who will plant and nurture the Torah even as he would a tree and who will devote all of his life, both physical and spiritual, to serve as its soil. ותומכיה And if a

7. Great is the Torah, for to those who find it it gives life in this world and in the world to come, as it is said: "For they are life to them that find them and health to all his flesh." And it is said: "It shall be health to your body and give marrow to your bones." And it is said: "It is a tree of life to those who maintain it, and those who lean upon it are a community that stride forward to salvation." And it is said: "They shall be a graceful garland about your head and necklaces around your neck." And it is said: "They give to your head a graceful garland and will allow you to forego a crown of glory." And it is said: "For by Me your days shall grow many, and the years of your life shall be increased." And it is said: "Length of days is in its right hand; in its left hand are riches and honor." And it is further said: "They shall add to you length of days and years of life and peace."

8. Rabbi Shimon ben Yehudah said in the name of Rabbi Shimon ben Yochai: Beauty, strength, riches, honor, wisdom, old age, a hoary head, and children are comely to the righteous and thus also for the world; as it is said: "The hoary head is a crown of glory; it is found

---

great many people will cleave to it, the Torah will form a bond, unifying the many into one single unit, prosperous and striding ever forward to salvation. לוית חן: It is through the Torah that your head, your mind and your understanding will gain the gift of Divine approval such as causes man's spiritual life to flourish. Then וענקים לגרגרותיך all your physical body, culminating in the neck that bears your head, will be so ennobled that the whole man shall come to honor. Once you have this Divine approval which rests upon your head and accompanies all of your spiritual endeavors, you will gladly forego any other crown of human glory. (תמגנך: "it will enable you to forego any other crown of glory") כי בי ירבו ימיך: Through תורה your days will last beyond the transient span of this life and even the years during which you dwell on earth will be turned for you into years of true living. אורך ימים בימינה: And if you seek nothing from the תורה but life eternal, as its gift to you from its "right hand", then it will endow you also with riches and honors with its "left hand" without your asking for it. It will render you rich by teaching you contentment, and it will bring you to honor by securing for you recognition from your fellow-men.

8. All the things enumerated here, which indeed comprise all that a man may desire, will be an ornament not only to him who possesses them but also to the entire world, if only the person having them will make use of them solely in the path of duty. עטרת תפארת שיבה: a "hoary head", the acquisition

בְּדֶרֶךְ צְדָקָה תִּמָּצֵא: וְאוֹמֵר תִּפְאֶרֶת בַּחוּרִים כֹּחָם וַהֲדַר
זְקֵנִים שֵׂיבָה: וְאוֹמֵר עֲטֶרֶת חֲכָמִים עָשְׁרָם: וְאוֹמֵר עֲטֶרֶת
זְקֵנִים בְּנֵי בָנִים וְתִפְאֶרֶת בָּנִים אֲבוֹתָם: וְאוֹמֵר וְחָפְרָה הַלְּבָנָה
וּבוֹשָׁה הַחַמָּה כִּי־מָלַךְ יְיָ צְבָאוֹת בְּהַר צִיּוֹן וּבִירוּשָׁלַיִם וְנֶגֶד
זְקֵנָיו כָּבוֹד: רַבִּי שִׁמְעוֹן בֶּן־מְנַסְיָא אוֹמֵר, אֵלּוּ שֶׁבַע מִדּוֹת
שֶׁמָּנוּ חֲכָמִים לַצַּדִּיקִים כֻּלָּם נִתְקַיְּמוּ בְּרַבִּי וּבְבָנָיו:

ט אָמַר רַבִּי יוֹסֵי בֶּן־קִסְמָא, פַּעַם אַחַת הָיִיתִי מְהַלֵּךְ בַּדֶּרֶךְ
וּפָגַע בִּי אָדָם אֶחָד וְנָתַן־לִי שָׁלוֹם וְהֶחֱזַרְתִּי לוֹ שָׁלוֹם. אָמַר
לִי, רַבִּי מֵאֵיזֶה מָקוֹם אָתָּה, אָמַרְתִּי לוֹ מֵעִיר גְּדוֹלָה שֶׁל
חֲכָמִים וְשֶׁל־סוֹפְרִים אָנִי. אָמַר לִי, רַבִּי רְצוֹנְךָ שֶׁתָּדוּר עִמָּנוּ
בִּמְקוֹמֵנוּ וַאֲנִי אֶתֵּן לְךָ אֶלֶף אֲלָפִים דִּינְרֵי זָהָב וַאֲבָנִים טוֹבוֹת
וּמַרְגָּלִיּוֹת, אָמַרְתִּי לוֹ אִם אַתָּה נוֹתֵן לִי כָּל־כֶּסֶף וְזָהָב וַאֲבָנִים
טוֹבוֹת וּמַרְגָּלִיּוֹת שֶׁבָּעוֹלָם אֵינִי דָר אֶלָּא בִּמְקוֹם תּוֹרָה, וְכֵן
כָּתוּב בְּסֵפֶר תְּהִלִּים עַל יְדֵי־דָוִד מֶלֶךְ יִשְׂרָאֵל טוֹב לִי תוֹרַת
פִּיךָ מֵאַלְפֵי זָהָב וָכָסֶף. וְלֹא עוֹד שֶׁבִּשְׁעַת פְּטִירָתוֹ שֶׁל אָדָם
אֵין מְלַוִּין לוֹ לְאָדָם לֹא כֶסֶף וְלֹא זָהָב וְלֹא אֲבָנִים טוֹבוֹת
וּמַרְגָּלִיּוֹת אֶלָּא תוֹרָה וּמַעֲשִׂים טוֹבִים בִּלְבָד, שֶׁנֶּאֱמַר בְּהִתְהַלֶּכְךָ

---

of long years of living, marks the old man as a person to whom honor is
due. But a hoary head as such is a mark of distinction only if the life of the
man has been a good and righteous one. Even as the hoary head lends dignity
to the old, so strength, not squandered in excesses, is an ornament to youth.
עטרת חכמים : Riches, too, are a crown, provided that it is a wise man whom
they adorn. עטרת זקנים : Grandchildren will be the crown of the old, if the
parents have been the pride of their children. If children have made it a matter
of pride to raise their offspring in the image of their own parents, then honest,
decent grandchildren will be the rewarding climax of their grandparents' lives.
וחפרה הלבנה : When the Kingdom of God will go forth from Jerusalem and
Zion, then His elders, who were the teachers and heralds of His Kingdom,

in the path of righteousness." And it is said: "The ornament of young men is their strength and the adornment of old men is a hoary head." And it is said: "The crown of the wise is their riches." And it is said: "Children's children are the crown of the old, and the adornment of children are their parents." And it is said: "The moon shall grow pale and the sun ashamed, for צבאות ה' has begun His reign in Mount Tzion and in Yerushalayim, and honor shall meet His elders." Rabbi Shimon ben Menasya, said: "These seven qualifications which the Sages enumerated as pertaining to the righteous were all realized in Rabbi [Judah the Prince] and in his sons.

9. Rabbi Yosé ben Kisma, said: I was once walking by the way when a man met me and greeted me. I returned the greeting. He said to me: "Rabbi, from what place are you?" I replied: "I come from a great city of sages and scholars." Thereupon he said to me: "Rabbi, if you would be willing to dwell with us in our place I would give you a million golden dinars and precious stones and pearls." I replied: "Were you to give me all the silver and gold and precious stones and pearls in the world, I would still not live anywhere except in a place of Torah." For thus it is also written in the Book of Psalms by David, the King of Israel, that "The teaching of Your mouth is worth more to me than thousands in gold and silver." Furthermore, when a man dies, neither silver nor gold nor precious stones nor pearls accompany him, but only the Torah and good works, for it

---

will shine forth in a splendor of spirit that will eclipse the physical light emanating from both sun and moon.

9. An explanation is still needed why Rabbi Yosé should have taken this inquiry as to his place of residence as a request to describe its nature. One might tend to think that מאיזה מקום אתה means "from what manner of place are you?". However, אי זה מקום denotes only the simple question "From what place...?". Cf. Sanhedrin 40a: באיזה שעה באיזה מקום. עמו במקומנו — "my towns-men are all all simple people like myself; they are not חכמים or סופרים." טוב לי etc. ולא עוד etc. The possession of the תורה is worth more and is more blissful than that of riches; it is immortal and thus remains with man even beyond the threshold of the grave where he has to leave behind all his other posses-sions. והקיצות: When you regain consciousness in the world to come, you will become conscious of such thoughts as you had originally derived from your study of the Torah while you were on earth.

תִּנְחֶה אֹתָךְ בְּשָׁכְבְּךָ תִּשְׁמוֹר עָלֶיךָ וַהֲקִיצוֹתָ הִיא תְשִׂיחֶךָ׃
בְּהִתְהַלֶּכְךָ תִּנְחֶה אֹתָךְ בָּעוֹלָם הַזֶּה בְּשָׁכְבְּךָ תִּשְׁמוֹר עָלֶיךָ
בַּקֶּבֶר וַהֲקִיצוֹתָ הִיא תְשִׂיחֶךָ לָעוֹלָם הַבָּא׃ וְאוֹמֵר לִי הַכֶּסֶף
וְלִי הַזָּהָב נְאֻם יְיָ צְבָאוֹת׃

י חֲמִשָּׁה קִנְיָנִים קָנָה (לֹו) הַקָּדוֹשׁ בָּרוּךְ הוּא בְּעוֹלָמוֹ וְאֵלּוּ
הֵן׃ תּוֹרָה קִנְיָן אֶחָד שָׁמַיִם וָאָרֶץ קִנְיָן אֶחָד אַבְרָהָם קִנְיָן אֶחָד
יִשְׂרָאֵל קִנְיָן אֶחָד בֵּית הַמִּקְדָּשׁ קִנְיָן אֶחָד׃ תּוֹרָה מִנַּיִן דִּכְתִיב
יְיָ קָנָנִי רֵאשִׁית דַּרְכּוֹ קֶדֶם מִפְעָלָיו מֵאָז׃ שָׁמַיִם וָאָרֶץ מִנַּיִן
דִּכְתִיב כֹּה אָמַר יְיָ הַשָּׁמַיִם כִּסְאִי וְהָאָרֶץ הֲדוֹם רַגְלָי אֵי־זֶה
בַיִת אֲשֶׁר תִּבְנוּ־לִי וְאֵי־זֶה מָקוֹם מְנוּחָתִי׃ וְאוֹמֵר מָה רַבּוּ
מַעֲשֶׂיךָ יְיָ כֻּלָּם בְּחָכְמָה עָשִׂיתָ מָלְאָה הָאָרֶץ קִנְיָנֶךָ׃ אַבְרָהָם
מִנַּיִן דִּכְתִיב וַיְבָרֲכֵהוּ וַיֹּאמַר בָּרוּךְ אַבְרָם לְאֵל עֶלְיוֹן קֹנֵה
שָׁמַיִם וָאָרֶץ׃ יִשְׂרָאֵל מִנַּיִן דִּכְתִיב עַד־יַעֲבֹר עַמְּךָ יְיָ עַד־יַעֲבֹר עַם־
זוּ קָנִיתָ׃ וְאוֹמֵר לִקְדוֹשִׁים אֲשֶׁר בָּאָרֶץ הֵמָּה וְאַדִּירֵי כָּל־חֶפְצִי־בָם׃

לי הכסף וגו': To the extent that the possession of material riches is good
and useful, and indeed, necessary for the fulfillment of the tasks set us by
the Torah, God Himself will grant us whatever in His wisdom He
deems necessary and desirable for us, without our having to pursue it ourselves
at the cost of the eternal values that the Torah affords.

10. Of all the Universe which is עולמו "His world" as a whole and in all
its parts, created and ruled by Him alone, the Lord has singled out five things
as His special possessions because they perform a special service to advance
the purposes of His Creation and His sovereignty. First there is the Torah, the
essence and the revelation of the purpose of His Kingdom on earth which it
is man's task to translate into reality. Then come heaven and earth as the
soil and the domain upon which the Torah is to be fulfilled. Then, Abraham,
as the cornerstone for the winning of mankind for the Kingdom of God;
Israel, as the messenger for the extension of the Covenant of Abraham to all
of mankind; and finally the מקדש, the Sanctuary of God and of His Law
which is to serve the preservation and advancement of Israel for this holy

is said: "When you walk it shall lead you; when you lie down it
shall watch over you, and when you awaken it shall address you."
"When you walk, it shall lead you"—in this world. "When you lie
down it shall watch over you"—in the grave. "And when you awaken
it shall address you"—in the world to come. And it is also said:
"Mine is the silver and Mine is the gold, says ה' צבאות."

10. Five possessions has the Holy One, blessed be He, declared
His own in this world: The Torah is a special possession; Heaven
and earth are a special possession; Abraham is a special possession;
Yisrael is a special possession; the Temple is a special possession. The
Torah: Because it is written: "God possessed me as the begin-
ning of His way before all His works, from of old." Heaven and
earth: Because it is written: "Thus says God: The Heaven is
My throne, the earth is my footstool; what manner of house will
you build for Me, and what manner of place for My rest?" And it is
written: "How manifold are Your works, O God; in wisdom have
You made them all; the earth is full of Your possessions." Abraham:
Because it is written: "Blessed be Avram to the Most High God, the
Possessor of heaven and earth." Yisrael: Because it is written: "Until
Your people pass over, O God, until the people whom You have
acquired pass over." And it is. written: "The holy ones that are on

---

purpose. ה' קנני ראשית דרכו Since it was the actual end for which the world
was brought into being, the concept of the Torah preceded Creation and was
employed by the Creator as the guiding standard for the Universe He made.
השמים כסאי וגו' But it was not only at one time, at their Creation, that Heaven
and earth were directly related to God, their Creator. Even now and forever-
more they are the throne of His dominion and the soil of His sovereignty.
Heaven is His throne from which, leading and guiding, He fashions the events
and phenomena of earth. The earth, in turn, is His footstool; all changes in
nature and history are but footprints of His progress through the ages. Tem-
ples and houses of worship are all only rooms used by men to gather to
worship the presence and sovereignty of God in heaven and on earth.
ברוך אברם לאל עליון Abraham is blessed not by God, but to God. The blessing
that is Abraham's serves to advance those purposes which God has set as
the goal of His sovereignty and which He seeks to bring about through His
guidance of Heaven and earth.
עם זו קנית: Israel had lost all those qualifications upon which its survival,

בֵּית הַמִּקְדָּשׁ מִנַּיִן, דִּכְתִיב מָכוֹן לְשִׁבְתְּךָ פָּעַלְתָּ יְיָ מִקְדָּשׁ אֲדֹנָי כּוֹנְנוּ יָדֶיךָ: וְאוֹמֵר וַיְבִיאֵם אֶל־גְּבוּל קָדְשׁוֹ הַר זֶה קָנְתָה יְמִינוֹ:

יא כָּל מַה־שֶּׁבָּרָא הַקָּדוֹשׁ בָּרוּךְ הוּא בְּעוֹלָמוֹ לֹא בְרָאוֹ אֶלָּא לִכְבוֹדוֹ, שֶׁנֶּאֱמַר כֹּל הַנִּקְרָא בִשְׁמִי וְלִכְבוֹדִי בְּרָאתִיו יְצַרְתִּיו אַף עֲשִׂיתִיו: וְאוֹמֵר, יְיָ יִמְלֹךְ לְעֹלָם וָעֶד:

רַבִּי חֲנַנְיָא בֶּן־עֲקַשְׁיָא אוֹמֵר, רָצָה הַקָּדוֹשׁ בָּרוּךְ הוּא לְזַכּוֹת אֶת־יִשְׂרָאֵל לְפִיכָךְ הִרְבָּה לָהֶם תּוֹרָה וּמִצְוֹת. שֶׁנֶּאֱמַר, יְיָ חָפֵץ לְמַעַן צִדְקוֹ יַגְדִּיל תּוֹרָה וְיַאְדִּיר:

קדיש.

---

both individual and national, depended, and it was only through direct Divine intervention in the course of history that the children of Israel became free as individuals and politically independent as a nation. By virtue of this act of God the people of Israel, both as individuals and as a group, became God's own possession forever, to serve to do His will and to advance His purpose on earth. All those who, with pure and complete devotion, live on earth for the realization of this their destiny are called by God, "His holy ones on earth." They do not shine forth in their own power and glory, but glory solely in the fact that God regards them as instruments for the fulfillment of His will. מכון לשבתך When the Lord apportioned the regions of earth among men, He retained for Himself, for a special purpose, one land ארץ ישראל, the Land of the Jews, which was to serve as the soil for His Law and of His people which was to live for the fulfillment of His Law. And within this one land He reserved for a special purpose one place, the Holy Mountain, to serve as the abode for the Sanctuary of His Law. From this place He would proclaim His presence and it was from this place, too, that the Law with its hallowing force was to win over, first Israel and then all the other nations of the world for God and for His Law. כי מציון תצא תורה ודבר ה' מירושלים.

earth, who are splendid by virtue of the fact that all My will is done through them." The Temple: Because it is written: "The place, O *God,* prepared for You to dwell in, which You, O *God,* have attained; the Sanctuary, O *God,* which Your hands have established." And it is written. "He brought them to the region of His Sanctuary, to this mountain, which His right hand had acquired."

11.   Whatever the Holy One, blessed be He, created in His world, He created solely for His glory, as it is said: "Everything that is called after My Name and that I have created for My glory I have formed and I have fashioned it." And it is said: "*God* shall reign for all eternity."

---

11. The teachings of wisdom of our "fathers" end with the thought that not only the Jewish people but, in fact, everything else that as a creation of God bears the Name of God, has no other purpose but to serve the Glorification of God, its Creator, Lord and Master. It is inevitable that all things should fulfill this destiny, for God has created each one of them especially for this purpose, and fashioned and guided it accordingly. The nature with which every creature is endowed at the time of its birth and all the influences that affect him under God's own guidance both have the ultimate goal to guide all things and all men along that path which will lead to the glorification of God alone on earth. ה' ימלוך לעולם ועד This thought appears already at the close of the שירת הים, the Song at the Reed Sea which beholds God in His workings. As we have indicated in the Commentary to Exodus 15:18, this may mean not only *"God* will reign throughout all the future to come," but also, and particularly in this context: "Some day in the future which may still be distant but is no less sure to come, God will reign as King over all mankind." (ibid.)

ק"כ

To Scott,
מזל טוב on your Bar Mitzah.
Mr. & Mrs. Leon Dworsky

D0094989